Self-Esteem

The Teen Girl's Journey to Self-Worth, Body Image, Mr. Right, and Being Your Whole You

Meagan Trayler

Acknowledgments

To my parents,

Mom and Dad, thank you for giving me wings to fly, I believe I can because of you

To my siblings,

Allison, Justus, Nina, Gretchen, and Summer

Each of you are amazing in your own unique way, thank you for all you add to our family, y'all will do incredible things

Zane,

You challenge me and sharpen me, and bring me back to solid ground,

Hadassah and Iridessa,

You light up my life with your unique sparkles, may you always be Somebodies

To all of you who have helped, given feedback, and shown up in the pages of this book,

Aunt Nessa, Elizabeth, Allison, Audrey, Kayla, Laura, Rachel, Courtney, Nina, Gretchen, and everyone else,

Thank You

To my God,

You're the only one who truly gives me the worth I crave, thank you for making me a Somebody

ISBN: 1984079212
ISBN-13: 978-1984079213

Contents

Introduction

I read something once which I've never forgotten. It said "Be Somebody, before you're Somebody's." That struck a chord with me and that chord has never left. I told someone once that, if I wrote a book, it would have to have one of two kinds of messages, either a message that I need to tell, or one that the world needs to hear. This book is both.

I have two daughters. They both are beautiful, intelligent, creative, and, often, hilarious. And the mistakes I've made I don't want them to make, too. If a person can learn from another's mistakes, there's no reason to make that mistake themselves. That's why I'm writing this book, so that every girl who reads it can learn from the mistakes I've made and the lessons I've learned, and be a stronger, healthier, whole person. That's what this book is about, becoming a whole person, through God, and in yourself.

As I'm writing this I'm 24 years old and, overall, very healthy. But as a teenager I struggled with self-esteem, confidence, and mental disorders – Obsessive Compulsive and depression. I was a perfectionist, a people-pleaser, and starving for affirmation and validation. All these things combined made me desperate for any kind of positive attention I could get. I was afraid I would never be good enough, because I never felt like I was. I didn't think a guy would ever like me. How could they, when I felt so unattractive? I had a loving family and very affirming parents, but as much as I drank in their affirmation, it wasn't enough. I had friends, talents, intelligence . . . the perfect environment in which to thrive. But that wasn't enough either.

Enter - a boyfriend. He was cute, confident, and he liked me! I clung to him like a leech. He gave me everything I didn't have, made me everything I wasn't. He gave me value, gave me worth, gave me confidence, gave me validation, made me good enough. He completed me and made me whole.

Except that he didn't, because he couldn't.

Chapter One

Be Somebody Before You're Somebody's

The Source of True Self-Worth

We were driving home together, for the first time, as a dating couple. He asked me, "So, you want to hold hands?" He offered me his hand. After a moment's hesitation, I took it. It was the first time I'd ever held a guy's hand before, and my stomach started doing gymnastics inside my core. The warm pressure of his hand on mine stayed with me for days, and it was all I could think about. I felt so valued, so seen, so *special*. I couldn't wait to see him again so I could feel like that some more. Being chosen, out of every other girl in the world, made me feel like I'd never felt before. I was worth something, apparently. I was actually desired. I was valuable. And it felt amazing.

What I didn't comprehend then, I understand now. What I didn't realize, not deep down in my heart of hearts, is that God has already given us innate value. I was already worth something. There was nothing I could do, and nothing my guy could do, to make me worth more than I already was. The same is true for you. There is nothing you can do, *nobody* who may say they love you, that will make you worth any more than you already are. A guy cannot give you worth because you are already worthy. Absolutely nothing can give you more worth than you already have.

In 1 John 4:10 it says "This is love: not that we loved God, but that he loved us and sent his Son as an atoning sacrifice for our sins" (NIV). You are worthy because . . . God. That's it. He made you, loves you, and died for you. Nothing you can do or attain can trump the God-given worth you have. And yet, we still struggle to accept it.

Here are some numbers for you.

- Ten thousand people a month google "Am I ugly?"[1]

- At any one time, 5% of teens suffer from major depression.[2]

- Over 5,000 teens a day, between ages 10 and 24, attempt suicide.[3]

Young people are trying to find their worth from sources that can never actually give them any real worth at all. They look for achievement to set them apart, which isn't wrong, but it can't give them the true value they crave. They work for the perfect body, hoping that that will make them "good enough" to be loved, accepted, or valued by others, but that doesn't give them the fulfillment they desire, either. They look to the person standing next to them, a boyfriend, girlfriend, or spouse, but they wind up empty. They don't realize, like I didn't, that people cannot give worth to other people. We look for our self-worth in all the wrong places, when there is really only one place we can truly find it.

Children, teens, and young adults are suffering, wanting to know they are loved and worthy, but they are looking to google or strangers on the internet to tell them they are valuable. There are numerous YouTube videos of people asking the online world if they are ugly or pretty. At prettyscale.com you can take an online test for a face beauty analysis and have your face analyzed in 3 minutes with a rating from 1-100. Many things can be found on the internet but *self-worth is not one of them*! When malicious people use their online presence destructively, someone else is sitting alone somewhere, crying in front of their phone screen, wishing that *someone* had said they are beautiful or valuable.

Some young people have no one speaking truth into their lives; no one who will talk about their innate worth. And so, when they look to a cruel cyber world for their value, they are left with a void ripe for depression, and if left unaddressed, self-harm or suicide. Something has to be done about this. Someone must do something. I am here to tell you that this is not the path to self-worth, and I can tell you what is . . .

Worth and value come from God. Simply because you are a human being you are worthy. Here's why: God is a spirit. God has given every human being a spirit. Spirits never die and that is what separates us from the rest of creation. God said "Let us make man in our image . . . " 4 We are created as representations, or images, of God. Animals and plants don't have spirits because they aren't made in the image of God. We step on ants and swat flies and never think a thing about it. But we all innately know that murder is wrong. Why? Because human lives have value. You are valuable, you are enough, simply because you are human, made in God's image. There's nothing you have to prove. There's nothing you have to change to be worthy. There's nothing you have to do to be valuable. You already are.

Let's say that someday one of my baby girls gets married. She might marry an amazing, wonderful guy. She'll be his and he'll be hers. But no matter how wonderful he is, he cannot make her Somebody if she isn't already. He can't give her enough affirmation, affection, or anything else, that'll make her "enough." If she doesn't realize that she is already innately valuable she'll look to him, as I did to my boyfriend, to determine her worth. But those things will never fulfill the need inside her to know that she is worthy. Her husband will never be able to bear the burden of her lack of self-esteem. It's too much for any individual to bear the load of someone else's self-esteem. Do you know what the great thing is? She already is enough. She's just got to own it, own the worth that God's already given her.

On top of being made in God's image, if you are a believer, God has adopted you and made you His child. You are the child of a God! What kind of crazy, wild, immense worth does that give you? It's almost too much to process in our limited minds. Sometimes we don't feel the worth we have. Sometimes God seems far away and we wonder if He still loves us, or is mad at us, and waiting to love us until we straighten up again. But God doesn't just put up with his children. He doesn't just tolerate our sin, hoping that someday we'll behave well enough for Him to have warm, fuzzy feelings for us. It's like this: God loves Jesus, yet, He still sent Jesus to die so He could bring us to Himself. He didn't need us, He just wanted us. Even though we behave badly, have rotten attitudes, forget to thank him, like to be rebellious, test his patience, and push His limits, He wanted us, and still does today. The Bible says He "delights" in us.5 He wanted us to be His so badly he allowed the Son he loves to die. *That* is what give us value.

We are the wildly loved children of a God. We are worthy and valuable and enough because of God. Made in His image and adopted as His daughters, we are enough. *You* are enough. When my baby girls have accepted these truths and really believe them, then they can be whole, complete people. Then they will be Somebody, and so will you.

Workbook

- Get a pen and paper and describe who and what you truly are in the light of your God-given worth. (I am worthy, I am valuable, I am a daughter of the King, I am loved, I am a conqueror, I am delighted in, . . .)

- Write this down: "I am enough."

- Write this down, too: "Be Somebody before you're Somebody's."

- Make a list of scriptures that describe who you are and how God sees you.

What They Said

What gets scary is when your self-worth is tied up in what strangers think of you.

- Emma Watson[6]

You alone are enough. You have nothing to prove to anybody.

- Maya Angelou[7]

Write It Down

1) Who truly gives you worth and value?

2) Have you really, in your deepest heart of hearts, embraced your innate worth?

3) Have you ever realized that you're "enough" just as you are and that you don't have to prove anything?

4) Do you see yourself as valuable?

5) Have you ever looked to another person to give you value and make you worthy?

6) What specifically resonated with you in this chapter?

7) Which Whole You Tips are you going to do today?

Notes

Chapter Two

Live For The Change
Pursuing Excellence

I imagined her in my mind. Constantly on her phone, all she did was take pictures of herself and text her friends alphabet soup: lol, jk, lmao, rofl, wya, idc, tgif. When she did actually look up and enter the real world, nothing she said had any real depth to it. Everything was about her, her friends, her weekend, the fun they were going to have, what so-and-so did last weekend, and the latest pictures of the hottest boy band that were circling the internet. All her social interactions were fits of giggling with her friends and flirting with the nearest available guy. I stared at her and tried to keep from rolling my eyes. *Is that it?* I wondered. *Is that really all you think about? There are really no big ideas floating around in that pretty head of yours? No dreams to do big things or change the world? Your future goes only as far as next weekend?*

Stagnation occurs when something, like a pool of water, is still, with no flow to it or from it. A stagnant body of water doesn't do anything. It doesn't feed a lake, or receive from a river, it just sits there. Whatever potential it has for giving life to other bodies of water is wasted.

Just like stagnant water, sometimes a person wastes their potential, because they aren't doing anything. They're set on cruise control going down the road of life. A stagnant person refuses to change and grow. This kind of person only knows what she knows and never learns anything new. She's too lazy to improve herself or work on a character flaw, and she may be stubborn and defensive about her lack of effort. She's passive, letting life slide by without actually doing anything productive. She piggy-backs off of other people's beliefs, not figuring out for herself what she believes. She's full of potential, but she's stagnant.

We don't want to be this girl. One thing that doesn't change, is that things will always change. We can choose to change also, into a stronger, Godlier person, or we can choose to be stagnant, wasting the time and potential God has gifted us. Our minds have an amazing capacity to learn and retain information. Our bodies are very versatile in the skills they can master. Each of us is unique in interests and tastes. These interests are directives God has wired into us to push us toward things we could excel in, and use to make a difference in the world. Not everyone is strong in the same areas, and that's okay. If God wanted us to be exactly the same, He'd have made us exactly the same. But He didn't. Instead of being carbon copies of each other, we are very different. Your talents and gifts will be different from someone else's. Whatever skills, interests, and talents you are blessed with, improve on those and figure out ways to use them for God's purposes.

A couple of examples: I have a sister who is an amazing writer. Right now, she is pursuing a degree in communications so she can continue to hone her craft and grow her skills. I strongly admire her commitment to growth and learning, and I also admire how she's using her skills to help people and glorify God. For instance, she's written and edited scripts for theater and film, that are clean and family-friendly, and written historical fiction based on the life of Christ. She has taken something she loves and is passionate about, writing, has continued to learn and grow in that passion, and found ways to bless others and praise God.

I also have a friend who has an amazing, and unusual, skill. She gives fantastic hugs! And I don't mean the sweet, gentle, sympathetic squeeze that people sometimes give you on a bad day. Her hugs are the I'm-so-excited-to-see-you, I'm-going-to-squeeze-you-until-you-suffocate, you-are-my-favorite-person-ever, type of hugs. I can't walk away from my friend without feeling better than I did before, and knowing that there is someone out there who loves me. And she does this for everybody! She has a love for people that is genuine, passionate, and contagious. It's extremely difficult not to like her. She gives what she has a talent for (among her many other gifts) a vivacious love of people through her amazing hugs.

Everyone is given something. If you think that you're not good at anything, you just haven't found what you like or are talented at yet. Try new things. Pick up a new hobby. Go to the library and browse the nonfiction section (I do that all the time!). Talk to someone who knows you well and see if they have ideas about what you might have an inclination towards. What are the things you most like to do? How can you become better at them? How can you bless people through them?

If you're the kind of girl who enjoys figuring things out and gravitates toward intellectual pursuits, pour yourself into that! If you love music and can't go a day without singing or playing an instrument, learn to do it proficiently. If you love art, sports, volunteering, drama, computer programming, caring for the sick, baking, whatever it is, learn to do it well and find a way to use it for God's glory, either by praising and pointing people to Him, or helping people and reflecting God's love to them. God can use you. You just have to be available to Him. Ephesians 2 says He's had good works planned for you to do since before you were born.

Everyone has been given gifts. What are yours? Are you a people-person? Compassionate? Encouraging? Wordy? Outdoorsy? Fashionable? Thrifty? Whatever it is, God can use it, and you.

I have another friend who feels called to serve others and love people in whatever way she can. For example, she's gone on a mission trip to Africa and helped rescue people in the wake of a destructive hurricane. I respect this girl very much because she has not only taken her life and calling seriously, she has used her time and talents for God and others and hasn't wasted them. Instead of thinking, "Oh, someone else will probably do it" she got out there and started helping, working and serving others. This is exactly what we need to be doing, using whatever we have, whether that's talent, money, energy, or simply our time and willingness, to give back. I asked her to write about her experiences in loving God and serving others. This is what she wrote:

> In a world where there is so much ugly, I feel the responsibility to spread beauty. Not only in my circle, my space, my comfort zone but everywhere. I believe two of the most beautiful things you can do in this world are to love and serve others. I often struggle with how to do this. So many times, I find myself only wanting to serve in "big ways" when serving small can make just as big of an impact.

> In 2013, Angelina Jolie was given the Jean Hersholt Humanitarian award. I remember standing in the kitchen with my almost-crying, watery eyes glued to the TV as she gave her acceptance speech. Something about it moved me. This is what she said...

> "My mother was very clear when she said, "Nothing would mean anything if I didn't live a life of use to others." I didn't know what that meant for a long time. I came into this business young and worried about my own experiences and my own pain. And it was only when I began to travel and look

and live beyond my home did I understand my responsibilities to others. When I met survivors of war and famine and rape, I learned what life is like for most people in this world and how fortunate I was to have food to eat, a roof over my head, a safe place to live and the joy of having my family safe and healthy. And I realized how sheltered I had been and I was determined never to be that way again. We are all, everyone in this room, so fortunate. I have never understood why some people are lucky enough to be born with the chance that I had, to have this path in life, and why across the world there is a woman just like me with the same abilities and the same desires, same work ethic and love for her family, who would probably make better films and better speeches. Only she sits in a refugee camp and she has no voice. She worries about what her children will eat, how to keep them safe and if they will ever be allowed to return home. I don't know why this is my life, and that's hers. I don't understand that, but I will do as my mother asked and I will do the best I can with this life. To be of use."

- Angelina Jolie

Being of use to others was something I had always had an interest in but I didn't really know how to go about it. I was only focused on the bigger ways to help and be of service. Because of this I didn't give it a whole lot of thought. There was something about her speech that brought the interest to serve others to the surface. Not only in big ways but in my everyday life. I felt it was something I needed to be doing as a Christian. And not just that, I wanted to.

In 2014 I was given the opportunity to go on my first ever mission trip to Kenya, Africa. I was ecstatic and also very nervous not knowing what to expect. My parents, especially my dad, did not want me to go because they felt I was putting myself at risk for danger. I didn't care. I was going to go and no one was going to stop me. While in Africa, a brother gave an amazing lesson that brought me to tears. It was on Isaiah

6:8 which says, "Then I heard the voice of the Lord saying, 'Whom shall I send? And who will go for us?' And I said, 'Here am I. Send me!'" God is looking for faithful men and women to accomplish His will and purpose on Earth. He uses willing and obedient servants, people who make themselves available to God's call upon their lives to build His kingdom. Everyone has a job to do and the way God uses you may be different from the way He uses me. He has a mission for all of us, but the question is whether or not we will accept the call and the talents He has given us to serve Him, to suffer for Him and to serve others. There are so many examples of faithful men and women in the Bible. They were ordinary humans just like you and I, but they were faithful and they let God do extraordinary things in their life. So many times I want to sit back and let someone else do the work. But I don't believe that's how God wants us to be. We should be bold and a shining light. I believe God wants us to say, "Here am I, send me!" Be willing to do whatever it is, whether big or small. Step out in faith.

There are so many ways to use our talents to serve others. We don't have to move to a third world country, although for some of us that might be the case. There are simple acts that can be done every day. You just have to be willing. In my prayers I ask God to open my eyes and heart to see opportunities around me to serve. I ask him to give me strength, boldness (because I am so shy) and a heart of compassion.

When I was in Colorado my family went out to eat one night at Olive Garden. Our waiter was a little shy but very nice and every time he would come to our table he would stay for a couple of minutes and we would talk about life or tell jokes. We ended up inviting him to my cousin's wedding the next day. At first he wasn't sure and didn't believe us. But throughout the dinner we continued to ask and encouraged him to come. By the end of the night he gave us his number and said, "If you are serious, text me tomorrow." Long story short, he came. His name was Mic. During the ceremony he cried. When I asked if he was okay he said, "I have never been around a family that puts so much emphasis on God and a relationship with Him. I did not come from that background." He came from a family that did drugs. He didn't know his mom and his dad wasn't around much. When he left that night he thanked us for inviting him, for allowing him to be a part of our family even if it was just for one night. He said that he felt loved and accepted. We really didn't do much. We invited him to the wedding and we treated him like we had known him all our life. We didn't know we were being examples but we were. Everyone has a story and you never know what people are going through. A simple hello, asking someone how their day is or inviting a stranger to be a part of something with you can change or make a big impact on someone's life. A lot of times we don't think these small acts of kindness matter but in today's world they go a long way.

Have you ever been through the drive through line and you get up to the window and they say, "Oh, the person in front of you paid for your meal. You don't owe anything." Doesn't that just make your day? Just a little act of kindness that can turn someone's day completely around. Opportunities are everywhere. Big and small. You just have to look and be willing.

She is right. Opportunities are everywhere and you just have to look and be willing. My friend is an awesome example of someone who has used what she had, her time, her energy, her resources, her talents, and her heart for service, and blessed others and glorified God. Sometimes it doesn't take much, only a willing heart. May we all be that person that says, "Here I am, send me!"

By always learning and growing in knowledge of something or skill in something, you will use and not waste the abilities God's given you. God has not given us talents and interests just to make life more fun. I believe the passions He's put inside you are paths to follow to loving people, loving yourself, and loving God. Those things are called ministry, fulfillment, and worship. For example, I love words and music, so I try to use those things to bless others and praise God. Whatever interests or talents you have, there's always a way to use them as blessings, instead of keeping them to yourself.

While writing this book has given me some qualms, I know I can use my love of words and language to, hopefully, help people. Though writing only for myself might be satisfying, it would only help me. But God has called us to love him and love others, not only ourselves. Shielding my gifts and talents from the world and hiding them under my bed might make me feel safe from scrutiny, but it isn't loving other people. It doesn't praise God. It only wastes the passions He's put inside me. So, I summon my courage, and I gather my talents and passions, and I put myself out there, to love others, love myself, and praise God. By doing that, I am continually growing and becoming better at the things I am passionate about.

I'm not saying there's anything wrong with doing things only for yourself that you enjoy, that's fulfillment, and I think that's a need God placed inside us. But only doing things for yourself is the path to selfishness. In Mark 12:33 we are called to love God, and love others as ourselves. That requires us to first love ourselves, so we can then love others. When you know that a God is kinda crazy about you, it's definitely a little easier to love yourself! God's love is where it all starts. He loves us like crazy, so we can love ourselves and others, because He does. It's a wonderful thing to do things that fulfill the needs and desires God's placed in your heart. Just remember, use them to bless others also.

When you continue to learn and grow, you'll also be more interesting as a person. Someone with diverse experiences and pursuits would have much more to offer in a conversation and life in general. The more you know about something, the more knowledge you can share with people. The more experiences you've had, the more information you can share with people. No one has the intention to be boring, but if we do nothing with our lives other than waste our time, that's eventually what we become! You're never too young to get better at something. You're never too young to learn more about something. With the amazing brains God's given us, we have the capacity to learn nearly anything we decide to.

Nerds are usually the people that are really, really into something. They love it, they spend time working on it, studying it, reading, or listening to it. Nerds are good at what they do because they've put in the time and effort. They enjoy it and it's important to them. People can be nerds about anything, such as electronics, books, or Star Wars. But I'm going to flip this around to the spiritual side. Are we nerds in our spiritual lives? Do we know why we believe what we believe? Do we even know what we believe or are we piggy-backing off of our parents' beliefs?

I was that girl once. Growing up, I was the goody-two-shoes who towed the line, said the right things, and followed the rules. But that can only last so long. Generally, a girl like that will either rebel, since there's no point in doing things she doesn't believe in anyway, or she'll "get real," searching for the truth in life for herself. That last one is what I want for you. Study what you believe. In a way, that's a form of rebellion too. Often, if someone's grown up in a religious home, spiritual things are taught to the children (as they should be!) but then those kids grow up, and continue doing what they've always done out of habit, or in fear of their parents' disappointed expectations, or for a similar reason. But if something is done by just going through the motions, not by conviction, or faith, or love, or belief, it is just an act. It's a lifestyle. That amounts to nothing, because it's insincere.

Now, I'm not saying you shouldn't do the right thing if you don't feel like it. We should always do what's right. But, do you actually know what's right? Have you read, and studied, and researched, and thought, and questioned until you have your own informed opinion on the subject? Have you asked the hard questions to people you trust? If someone asks you a question about a spiritual topic, do you know how to find scriptures, do word searches, look at the original language, use a chain-reference, Bible website, or Bible app? Are you nerdy about what you believe?

I didn't use to be, but I really try to now. It's a struggle sometimes and it's always a process. But I've found that the more I decide for myself the convictions I hold, the stronger in my faith and the more confident I am. No one can take us to Heaven. No one can drag us to Heaven. We aren't just going to fall in, get lucky, do enough good things, or pray the "right" prayer. The Christian faith is an active one. It's the search for truth.   If I don't learn and grow in the truth, and if you don't learn and grow in the truth, what point is there in growing in any other area? The search for truth is the most important search in our entire lives. If we fail to find the truth, we've failed in everything.

A part of growing in the truth is growing our characters in Godly attributes. Many people are lazy in this area, too. They'll say, "I was born this way," translation - "I shouldn't have to work on my flaws because I can't help having these weaknesses." Or they'll say, "I'm just a work in progress," translation - "I'm not too great, but I'm not that bad either, so I'll just stay how I am because I'm perfectly comfortable this way." To these people I really want to sound a gong and say "Wake up call!" Having a weakness is no excuse for not trying to improve it. Having a short temper doesn't mean you shouldn't take a deep breath and count to ten when someone is pushing your buttons. Having a tendency to bully others doesn't mean you shouldn't stop and try to see things from the other person's perspective, and then respond to them with respect and kindness. Being born with weaknesses makes someone human, it's not an excuse to avoid strengthening character.

When we become God's kid, He gives us His Holy Spirit, which includes His attributes. But just because He's given us His Spirit doesn't mean we don't have to *try* to have His attributes. It just means they're ours for the taking if we want them. God's not going to force us to be gentle when we want to be rude, or patient when we want something right-now-this-minute. But He will give us the nudge to do what is right, and the strength and self-control to do it. The weaknesses that are innate to us can be improved by the strengthening of our Godly attributes. When I am frustrated and impatient, oftentimes I can feel the God-sent nudge to be gentle and kind. It's hard to respond to sometimes, and I don't always get there, but sometimes I do. Those are the victories. The times when I really want spit out the awesomely rude, sarcastic remark that's headlining in my brain, I feel the nudge to bite it back, and keep my mouth shut. I'm sure that people wonder sometimes if my silence is agreement with what they have to say (or maybe evidence of an empty head!) but really, it's my self-control holding back a stinging, honest reply. I may say a lot sometimes, but I don't say a whole lot more. Those are the victories. And for the failures, there's grace. Loads and loads of grace. The Bible says that God's mercies are new every morning. That means there's enough grace to cover all my failures for that day. And then the next day, there's more grace to cover all those failures, too.

It seems like, sometimes, when someone becomes a Christian, they think they've crossed the finish line, they're done. But really, that's only the beginning. There is so much to learn and so many ways to grow! Even more mature Christians, who are experienced in the faith, sometimes get passive. By forgetting to grow they start becoming close-minded and stubborn in their beliefs and their character. It shouldn't be like that. In 2 Peter 1 it says -

> [M]ake every effort to add to your faith virtue; and to virtue, knowledge; and to knowledge, self-control; and to self-control, perseverance; and to perseverance, godliness; and to godliness, brotherly kindness; and to brotherly kindness, love. For if you possess these qualities and continue to grow in them, they will keep you from being ineffective and unproductive in your knowledge of our Lord Jesus Christ.

Everyone has the responsibility to own their faith and their character. Everyone has the responsibility for self-improvement and personal growth. Hebrews 6:1 says "Therefore let us move beyond the elementary teachings about Christ and be taken forward to maturity . . ." If something's not going up, it's falling down. Faith and character don't just happen, they are created and cultivated. And the only person that can do that for you is you. But that's the great thing! You own your spirituality, you own your convictions, your beliefs, and your knowledge. No one can take that away from you. Once you've owned them, they're yours. Grow in knowledge, skill, and Godliness. They're yours for the taking.

Workbook

<u>Whole You Tips</u>

- List things that you're good at.

- Choose one that you want to improve in and make it a goal.

- Write down some topics you want to learn more about.

- List some character traits that you're strong in.

- Choose a character trait that needs improvement and make it a goal.

- Describe how you can use these strengths and character traits to fulfill yourself, minister to others, and glorify God.

<u>What They Said</u>

Learn from the mistakes of others. You can't live long enough to make them yourself.

- Eleanor Roosevelt[1]

Great minds discuss ideas, average minds discuss events, small minds discuss people.

- Eleanor Roosevelt[2]

To Live is the rarest thing in the world. Most people exist, that is all.

- Oscar Wilde[3]

Being realistic is the most commonly traveled road to mediocrity.

- Will Smith[4]

Continuous effort - not strength or intelligence - is the key to unlocking our potential.

Winston Churchill[5]

Write It Down

1) Are you intentional about learning and improving yourself?

2) What is one area you'd like to grow and improve in?

3) Do you ever think about strengthening your character?

4) Are you a nerd in your spiritual life?

5) What do you do now to help yourself grow spiritually?

6) What specifically resonated with you in this chapter?

7) Which Whole You Tips are you going to do today?

Notes

Chapter Three

You're The Only You
Embracing Your Uniqueness

I couldn't stand it. My little sister was so gorgeous. She was everything a budding young woman was supposed to be, and she got the attention to prove it. She was cool, attractive, fashionable, and irritatingly beautiful. I wanted those big, brown eyes, full lips, and buoyant hair. But what I wanted most was her insane quality of attractiveness. Why did everyone like her? Why did guys line up to talk to her? (Not really, but they might as well have.) Why couldn't I be like that? While she was off being cool and getting attention, I was over here feeling frumpy and awkward. It wasn't fair. If only I could change myself, if I could be more pleasing and attractive somehow, maybe people would like me, maybe I'd get attention, too. If I made myself different, if I weren't exactly *me*, maybe I'd be acceptable.

There is no one else exactly like you. You are unique. I am unique. Yet, sometimes we're afraid to be ourselves. Maybe that's because we're afraid of what people will think of us, we're afraid they won't like us, or we don't think we're good enough just as "us." Maybe we want that certain person to like us, or be our friend, so we change ourselves trying to be someone we're not. I've tried to be witty so people will think I'm funny, and then like me. But I'm really not very witty at all, so my attempts usually flop. I've tried to change things about myself for someone else, but it never lasts. When you try to change yourself for someone else, either out of pressure to please them or in desperation to "keep" them, it isn't genuine. If something isn't real, if it isn't meaningful to you, it won't last. Because if something is only half-hearted, there's no real commitment.

I'm a pleaser by nature. I like people to be happy and I like to make them happy. I also hate disapproval and confrontation. I get so nervous when I think someone is upset with me or that there might be a confrontation, that I tremble, my neck muscles freeze up, and I get tension headaches. Then, I find myself running around trying to be Little Miss Perfect, doing everything exactly right (like that's actually possible), leaving the thermostat alone in case someone wouldn't like it changed, avoiding topics that might cause disagreements, keeping my kids quiet so no one snaps at us, trying to do everything I can think of to keep people happy so I won't be uncomfortable or have to deal with their displeasure.

But am I "comfortable" running around trying to be perfect when that's impossible? Am I responsible for someone else's happiness or anger? Am I everyone's Miss Manager of Emotions? Should I frantically be trying to change who I am to avoid someone else's negativity, or to stay in a relationship? No. God made me unique and made you unique for a reason. He called us to be like him, not each other. In 1 Peter 1:16 He said "be holy like I am holy". Changing my personality, my likes and dislikes, or beliefs for someone else is dishonest.

Working to change character, though, is something altogether different. We ought to be trying to improve our characters with Godly attributes. Also, when we're convicted by scripture we must always change accordingly. That is being holy like God is holy. Trying to change our negativity to joy or apathy to goodness, for example, is spiritual fruit that God is pleased with.

Changing who we are or what we believe for somebody else, instead of from personal conviction, is insincere, and most likely won't last very long. I heard an older man talking along these lines one time and he basically said that changing yourself for someone else usually only lasts about a year. Looking back on experiences in my life, I see that's true.

You are who you are *on purpose*! Don't let someone manipulate you into changing your very personhood, what makes you you. Let people challenge you, let them inspire you, let them teach you, let them advise you, let them be an example that you are willing to follow. But don't change yourself just to please another person. If they were to fall off of a mountain and die tomorrow, the world would not stop turning. They are just people. Change your character to be like God's, but don't change the uniqueness he gave you. It's a gift. It makes you one of a kind, and one of a kind is very valuable.

A caveat here. This doesn't mean we should purposefully continue doing things that irritate people because we refuse to change ourselves for them. For instance, if I'm in the habit of constantly interrupting people and I refuse to work on it when it's brought to my attention, that's just rude and disrespectful. Or, if someone doesn't like to be touched very much, aside from the polite handshake and the like, it'd be courteous to respect that person's wishes. If your parents want you to keep your room clean, refusing to clean it is disrespectful to them. Use discernment and courtesy. Embracing your personality and temperament is one thing, being stubborn and rude is another. There is no excuse for being a disrespectful person. Everyone else is unique, valuable, and worthy, too, and we should treat them that way. Embrace how God made you, and invest in your Godly character. That will give you self-respect and dignity, and that's wonderful to be around.

God made you you. So be her! If you love electronics, horses, books, working out, whatever it is, then love those things! There is no reason to change who you are to please someone else. If they don't like you for you, as long as you're growing your character in Godliness, then it's their loss. Some personalities just don't gel, and that's perfectly okay. God gave you your personality and interests for his personal reasons. Take those things and use them to glorify him. You don't have to be like anyone else. They don't have to be like you. You aren't them and vice versa.

Don't be a lemming.

You're totally unique.

Own it.

Are you a people-person? Make lots of friendships and reflect Christ in them. Are you shy? Write people notes telling them the things you admire about them. Do you enjoy holding babies? Look for a young mom at church who has her hands full and offer to give her a break for a few minutes. She'll probably be grateful you asked!   Be yourself. God can use that.

A few of the interests I have are books, nutrition, music, writing, and tea parties. I love to read and I love to share books and my thoughts about them with other people. I'm very interested in nutrition, so making healthy snacks and meals for me and my family has become a hobby. I also love having tea parties. There's just something so elegant and refined about a tea party! I've tried to bless people by making them for friends' birthdays, or just to break up the monotony of the daily routine. It's also a special common interest I share with my daughters. There's always some way to take what you enjoy and use it to bless others or glorify God. Sometimes, it may just take a little imagination to figure out how.

It's taken me a long time to embrace who I am and how God made me. My younger self was probably the most jealous person you'd ever meet. I wanted every good quality that everyone else had, especially the physical ones. It wasn't enough that I'd been given good qualities and talents, too, I wanted everyone else's plus mine. If she was thin, I wanted to be thin. If she was popular, I wanted to be popular. If she was outgoing, I wanted to be outgoing. If she was good at such-and-such, I wanted to be good at it, too. But I forgot one thing, to embrace who I, myself, was. It wasn't until recently that I really started doing that. I began respecting myself, standing up for myself, learning about myself, challenging myself, unapologetically being me and doing the things that "me" likes to do.

I like to read fiction and nonfiction books. I like to sing high and loud. I need solitude. I'm better at interacting with small groups, or one on one, than with large crowds. I have dreams, and with only one life to live I'm going to reach for them. I'm a Highly Sensitive Person.[1] I have a passion to mentor young women. My Love Languages are Words of Affirmation and Acts of Service.[2] I love to challenge myself intellectually. I want to help and minister to people. Nutrition is important to me, and so is chocolate. I want to travel the world. I prefer yoga to running. I like dim or natural lighting. I like my hot beverage first thing in the morning. I've got fair skin, wavy hair, and a high forehead. I'm a committed dreamer. I'm a visionary. I see how things could be, not just how they are. I'm Meagan, and I'm okay with that.

The more I've learned about who I am, the easier it has become to embrace who I am and love myself. Learning about yourself is probably a lifelong project. You'll learn more things about yourself as you gain knowledge, have new experiences, meet people, and develop skills. It's a wonderful and fulfilling experience to learn about and embrace who you are, because really, can you actually be anybody else? It's freeing to be able to say "I know who I am, and I'm okay with it."

Here's a little project for you: figure out who you are. What makes you, you? What makes you tick? What causes you to jump for joy? What pushes your buttons? What needs do you have? What are the best ways to take care of yourself? In what environments do you operate the best? What lights your fire? What do you want to leave behind? Learning to embrace who you are is important. You'll never be anybody else.   Whatever intricacies that are unique to you are there on purpose. Discover them, and then embrace them. Once you do, find ways to challenge yourself. Find things you want to be good at. Look for someone to invest in. Search for ways to make the world more beautiful. These pursuits will give your life personal passion and purpose. Only within the realms of knowing and embracing who you are, and loving God, and blessing others, will you find true joy and fulfillment. In Psalm 37:4 it says to delight yourself in the LORD, and he will give you the desires of your heart. What are the desires of your heart?

Maybe you know how to be yourself, but what if you don't really *like* yourself? Maybe we don't like how we look, or an aspect of our personality. Maybe we think we're "too" something: too tall, too short, too loud, too quiet, too bookish, too curvy, too thin, too muscular, too dramatic. Or, maybe we think the opposite. Perhaps we think we're not "enough" something, not smart enough, not pretty enough, not cool enough, not attractive enough, not "enough" enough. I've felt that way. I've wasted plenty of time criticizing my appearance, griping about what other girls have "enough" of that I don't, and wishing my personality were different.

But what good does berating ourselves really do? Why do we cut ourselves down? Is it making us better people? No, it only makes us more negative and zaps our joy. Maybe we think we're being humble, but that's not true. Humility is thinking of others, not bashing yourself. I've read somewhere that "humility isn't thinking less of yourself, it's thinking of yourself less." Life can be really hard sometimes, why make it harder by being your own personal bully? We girls are often very good at this. It somehow feels holy to down ourselves, as if that is pleasing to God. Nothing could be further from the truth! God loved you enough to make you his kid, he loves you as you are, as he created you. Downplaying what he created, died for, and loves, is an insult to him. There's nothing humble or holy about it. Let's stop this! There's absolutely no reason to make life more difficult for ourselves by being our own worst enemy.

I've got another challenge for you: like yourself. If *you* don't like you, how will anyone else? It's not humble to dislike yourself, nor is it attractive. Determine, for your sake, for the sake of those who love you, and for God's glory, that you will work on embracing your uniqueness. And I don't mean feed your already outrageously inflated ego, if you have one. I do mean recognize your true identity as a loved and chosen daughter of the King. Relish the gifts he's given you that you can use to fulfill yourself, bless others, and worship him. Accept and appreciate the uniqueness of your personality and characteristics and grow in confidence, learning who you are and deciding who you want to be. Figure out your strengths, talents, and weaknesses, and then use your strengths, develop your talents, and improve on your weaknesses. Discern just who you are, and love her! You're amazing. You're loved. You're unique. You're one in the history of ever! Practice loving yourself. I've got a couple of tips to help you do this.

If you're in the habit of self-criticizing or negative self-talk, practice recognizing those thoughts, and then replacing them with a positive one. If you catch yourself criticizing a personal feature you don't particularly like, for instance, dismiss that thought and replace it with a thought of a feature you do like. For example-

Me, thinking, in front of the mirror- *Meagan, your forehead is so huge, you could paint a picture on it.*

- Oops. I was doing it again. Okay, positive thought, positive thought.

- Why can't I be tan like other girls? I look like a ghost in winter. Snap! I was supposed find a positive thought. Okay, ummm. . .

- Oh, what I wouldn't give for long, dark, luxurious, actually-able-to-see-them eyelashes . . .

-Argh, this is hard!

- Okay, here we go. . .

-Meagan, those natural highlights in your hair are very pretty. People pay money for those and you get them free!

- Thank you, self. I appreciate you noticing for once.

- Oh, it's nothing.

- But it is, you know that.

- Yes, yes, I know. Loving you is never nothing.

It's not prideful. It's healthy. Getting out of the downward spiral of negative self-talk is difficult, but so necessary to living a balanced, healthy life. It's in the mind that battles are won and lost. Taking ownership for our thought lives is the first step to victory.

Maybe liking yourself isn't something you struggle with. If not, that's great! A healthy view of self is something very valuable. It's called self-esteem, and unfortunately for many girls, it can be a major struggle. I know someone who replaces the term "self-esteem" with "God-confidence". I love that! Self-esteem is what we think about ourselves. But when we take to heart what the God of the universe thinks of us, it's so much easier to be confident and embrace who we are.

A large part of loving self (and others, too) is acceptance. To unconditionally love someone is to accept who they are, and love them anyway. Accepting ourselves seems counterintuitive. Accept myself? Shouldn't I NOT accept myself? Isn't that being lazy, prideful, or settling for mediocrity? No, please understand, accept yourself not *as* you are, but *who* you are. As has been mentioned previously, each of us has a personal responsibility to learn and grow. But, we also have the responsibility to accept who we are, who God made us to be, with our own unique personality and personhood, so we can live healthy, Godly lives. A house divided against itself cannot stand, according to Mark 3:25. If we're continually fighting against ourselves, we're going to lose. We'll lose our ability to promote a healthy self, lose our good influence on others, lose our availability for God to use us, lose peace of mind, lose our power to pursue a fulfilling, purposeful future. Not accepting ourselves is accepting defeat. Satan uses any ploy he can to pull us away from God. I think he targets girls and women, especially, to poison our minds with lies about worth, self-esteem, body image, confidence, and beauty. These issues are central to womanhood. Each of us longs to know we are worth something, that we and our bodies are beautiful, admired, and appreciated, that we can truly know, deep down, that we are acceptable, and can be confident in that. The thing is, God has already told us all those things in his Bible. He's told us we are beautiful, worthy, accepted, delighted in, and loved. So, why is it so hard for us to accept ourselves? The God of the universe is crazy about us. We need to give ourselves a break and say, "You know what, maybe I'm not exactly how I wish I were, but I'm pretty awesome how I am. Since my perfect God loves and accepts me, I'm going to love and accept me, too."

When I was envious of my sister for everything she had that I didn't, I couldn't accept myself for who I was. When I focused on her pros and my cons, I was letting Satan win. She was beautiful, yes, she had all the amazing qualities I craved, and more. But I ignored all the amazing qualities that God had given me. My sister is amazing. She's got a heart much more beautiful than her face, and her face is gorgeous. She's never flaunted anything in my face, she's always been there for me when I needed her. So, my bitter, envious heart was a reflection on me, not her. If I would have accepted myself, and learned to cultivate and like myself, then I'd have been able to embrace all the beautiful things in her, instead of coveting them. Accept yourself for who you are . . . and then like her. Let me tell you from experience, it's worth it.

What if you don't think you actually *can* accept yourself? What if you've got some major struggles or addictions that you're dealing with? Accepting yourself doesn't mean accepting addictions or anything like that. Absolutely not. If there are things that need to be dealt with and gotten rid of in your life, do it! If something is plaguing you, or destroying your peace and health, it must be gotten under control. Get help, go to a parent or safe adult, make a plan, get counseling, do whatever needs to be done to get whole and healthy. Depression, anxiety, mental disorders, eating disorders, cutting, self-harm, abuse, if these things or things like this have infiltrated your life, please get help and pursue healing. According to National Alliance on Mental Illness (www.nami.org)

"20% of youth ages 13-18 live with a mental health condition." You are not alone. I've dealt with some of these things and I know others who have, too. You are not the only one. If you are dealing with any kind of disorder or self-harm please get help. I am not a physician, but I know from experience and study, that these things can be dangerous and destructive if left unaddressed. You are worth the journey to health and healing. Get help now.

While we must learn to love and accept ourselves to live whole, healthy lives, something we absolutely cannot accept in ourselves is sin. Of course, we're all going to mess up sometimes, say something we shouldn't, or lash out in anger. But I'm talking about a continual habit of sin, in other words, rebellion. Rebellion, sinful rebellion, is defiance against God. Rebellion of tradition, cultural norms, etc., is totally different. But rebellion against God is a very scary and dangerous place to be. We don't want to be there. God doesn't take pride off of us, and rebellion is, in essence, us telling God that we know better, we don't care, or we're going to do things our own way. That's the wrong thing to tell an all-powerful Being who could incinerate the world with a mere thought. God is patient and loving and kind, as the Bible says, and at the same time He is jealous, just, and a consuming fire.[3] And you don't play around with fire.

A habit of sin could be active, purposeful rebellion, or it could just be a lack of improvement in an area that you're weak in. Not trying to get stronger in a weakness is the same as accepting a weakness. Continuing to sin because it's easy for you is still sin. Being whole, healthy, and Godly, dictates that we continually strengthen our characters, accepting ourselves, but never accepting sin. Gossip is a big one with a lot of girls, bullying is another. Maybe you struggle with pride and vanity. Maybe disrespecting your parents, being rude and sarcastic, is a habit you've gotten into. Perhaps it's gluttony, over indulging until you've made yourself sick.

Think about your habits. Are they good habits or bad habits? Sinful or Godly? Do you encourage and affirm people, or do you criticize and tear people down? Are your words and tones respectful and kind, or do they reek of bad attitudes and defiance? Is social media a way you maintain friendships and share the highlights of your life, or is it a means to bully other girls, telling them things you'd never say to their faces? Habits can be easy to fall into, and hard to get out of, if they're bad or passive habits. Good habits require effort and intention, but they're so worth it! For example, practice encouraging others and speak well of them, instead of talking about them behind their backs. It's an investment that will last a lifetime. Not only will it bring you satisfaction, it will bring joy to those around you. Consider your habits and attitudes, and determine if there are areas of your life where you've cultivated some active or allowed some passive rebellion.

If reflection and self-evaluation is new or difficult for you, ask someone you trust for their perspective. They might be able to show you a tendency or weakness in you that's hard for you to see yourself. This takes humility. If you approach someone for their point of view, be sure to receive what they say humbly without getting defensive. After all, when you want to become stronger as a person, sometimes it takes hearing and doing hard things. But it's honorable. The strongest people weren't born that way, they became that way. Strengthening yourself will not only give you the respect of others, you will respect yourself more too.

While it may be difficult at first, self-reflection is a very valuable skill to possess. Some people have very little self-reflection skill and they can hardly see past the end of their own noses. They can never see when they're wrong, much less admit it. It's always someone else's fault, they don't apologize for anything, and they can be very difficult and frustrating to deal with. Let's not be that person! Being able to honestly look at yourself and know you've messed up, sincerely apologize for it, and work to avoid that error in the future, is a priceless, valuable, and Godly muscle that will serve you well. You will earn the esteem of others for your vulnerability and integrity, you will be easy to approach because you have a teachable, humble spirit, and your confidence will grow because you have nothing to be ashamed of, since you've taken care of every mistake you've made as best you could. Self-reflection and humility go hand in hand, but so do satisfaction and confidence. It takes humility to realize and admit a wrong and to make it right. It brings you satisfaction and increases confidence, though, when you know you've done well, acted appropriately, handled a situation skillfully, or maintained your self-control.

You're the only you, so be yourself. Like yourself. You have an intricate personality and totally unique personhood. You're full of minute details that make you, you. Don't be afraid to be different, that's who you are. No two people are exactly the same. Why should we try to be just like someone else when we absolutely can't? If we respect and admire someone, of course we can emulate them and follow their good example. But to try to be just like someone else, when you're totally unique and handcrafted by God, is pointless. You're not them, you're you! Embrace who you are, make yourself as strong and amazing, as passionate and Godly, as you can be. You won't regret it. Living your own life with passion and dedication to the purposes God has called you to, and the confidence that he loves you and has given you what you need to fulfill those purposes, is not a waste or bore, but a thrilling adventure. As long as who you are and what you do is God honoring, it's all good! Don't try to become somebody else. Become the best version of you that you possibly can. You're a fantastic person to be. Be her!

Workbook

<u>Whole You Tips</u>

- Make a list of things you love about yourself, include attributes of your body, character, personality, and overall uniqueness.

- What is something that makes you unique and different from your family or your friends? Own this trait and use it in a positive way.

- What is a character trait that you are really strong in? Find Bible verses that talk about this trait.

- How can you fulfill yourself, bless others, and glorify God, with your unique personality and gifts?

<u>What They Said</u>

Why fit in when you were born to stand out?

- Dr. Suess[4]

In order to be irreplaceable, one must always be different.

- Coco Chanel[5]

She woke up every morning with the option of being anyone she wished. How beautiful it was that she always chose herself.

- Tyler Kent White[6]

I can't think of any better representation of beauty than someone who is unafraid to be herself.

- Emma Stone[7]

Write It Down

1) Do you like who you are?

2) If not, what are you doing to change that?

3) Have you ever tried to change yourself to please or "keep" someone else?

4) Have you accepted yourself, your personality, strengths, weaknesses, quirks, talents, body type, and unique personhood?

5) Are there things that need to be dealt with or gotten rid of in your life?

6) Have you cultivated any active, or allowed any passive, rebellion against God?

7) What resonated with you about this chapter?

8) Which Whole You Tips are you going to do today?

Notes

Chapter Four

Healthy is the New Beautiful
Nourishing Mind, Body, and Spirit

I was sitting in the car beside my mom, sobs wracking my body. I hadn't meant to cry like this. But the more I talked the more envious and hopeless I felt. Why couldn't I be like that girl? She was so slender, and she had a boyfriend, so of course, those things went together. I could just imagine that if he put his arm around her, her waist would swim around in the crook of his elbow. Why couldn't I be that petite? Wouldn't I have a boyfriend, too, if I were? Why did I have to look like me? Why couldn't I be as slim and attractive as her?

I've felt those feelings many times, about many different people. There's always someone who seems to have it better or have it more: the allure, the body, the beauty. Even now, when I look around at the women I see in my life, I can immediately feel those feelings again. I feel small and less than. But what I've come to realize is that a lot of those girls that seem to have it all, the looks, the body, the confidence, the attention, they often struggle with the same feelings that I do. They struggle with body image, self-esteem, and confidence, too. We're all in this womanhood thing together. We feel the same emotions, struggle with the same issues, wish for the same attractive qualities. When I'm sitting there wishing I looked like her, there's probably someone else sitting there that's wishing she looked like me. It's so silly! Wouldn't it be incredibly boring if every woman in the world had the exact same face? Even if that face were the most gorgeous thing you've ever laid eyes on, it'd get old really fast. I've learned that the more I embrace who I am and how I look, and the more I champion and affirm other women, the less hold those feelings have on me. Because (besides the ridiculous beauty pageants people hold) this isn't a competition. We aren't running against each other to win anything. There are wonderful, beautiful qualities about you that I probably don't have, and vice versa. Embrace those things, give yourself a compliment, and while you're at it, compliment another girl, too.

The world has many ideas about what beautiful means, and it's always changing. Sometimes it means curvy, sometimes slender, sometimes it means tan skin, sometimes fair, sometimes it means lavish makeup, sometimes it means a natural look. There are so many messages the culture throws at us in this very sensitive area of beauty. Beauty brands have slogans. Ads have taglines. Magazines toss you hooks in the checkout line. It just. Doesn't. Stop.

I'm not going to sift through all these messages or tell you to completely ignore them, because that's practically impossible. But I will pose a question to you - "What is your definition of beauty?" Beauty is, and can be, many different things. I don't believe it's right to limit something as vast and universal as beauty to only certain things like tan skin, big breasts, and large eyes. Yes, all those things are beautiful, but so are many other things. I love Emma Watson's perspective on beauty.

Beauty is not long hair, skinny legs, tanned skin or perfect teeth. Believe me. Beauty is the face of who cried and now smiles, beauty is the scar on your knee since you fell when you were a kid, beauty is the circles when love doesn't let you sleep, beauty is the expression on the face when the alarm rings in the morning, it's the melted makeup when you have a shower, it's the laughter when you make a joke you're the only one who can understand, beauty is meeting his gaze and stopping understanding, beauty is your gaze when you see him, it's when you cry for all you[r] paranoias, beauty is the lines marked by time. Beauty is what we feel in the inside which also shows outside us. Beauty is the marks the life leaves on us, all the kicks and the caresses the memories leave us. Beauty is letting yourself live.

Isn't that so perfect and poignant? How can we restrict beauty to only certain things in a world full of variety, vibrancy, and wonder?! Beauty is too vast to be so limited. Let us try to embrace beauty in all its many forms.

I want to suggest to you one thing in particular that is, I believe, a key and very important element of beauty: health. When I say health, I don't mean it as in not being sick, but health, as in maintaining a healthy lifestyle. There was a time that I really only cared about being skinny. I couldn't have cared less how active I was, nor did I care much about balanced nutrition, as long as I didn't gain any weight. But when I was 23 years old I started doing yoga frequently, as well as other forms of exercise. I haphazardly picked up some books on health and nutrition at the library, and as I read, my knowledge increased and my perspective about what it means to eat a healthy diet changed. After that, I continued to read books on healthy eating, and I continued to practice yoga. Mainly as a result of these two habits, my lifestyle shifted in a very beneficial way.

Since then, I've tried to eat a lot more whole foods, many of those being plant-based foods. I also try to exercise semi-frequently. When I do these things consistently, I noticeably feel better, and too, because I know I'm being kind to my body, I feel better emotionally as well. It's all connected. Because the mind directs the body, and the body houses the mind, the health of one affects the other. So, healthful improvement in one will definitely influence the other. Whole foods is, basically, food as it's meant to be eaten, minimally or unprocessed, in as natural a form as possible without a bunch of fake stuff in it. I love eating fruit and vegetables and whole grains like oatmeal and brown rice, for example. Eating foods in their natural, or close to natural state allows them to retain optimal amounts of nutrients. I've also cut down on white sugar in certain parts of my diet, like in my coffee and cereal, as granulated sugar is terrible for the body.   I'm not great at limiting processed sugars. I've got a ginormous sweet tooth and I love baked goods with a voracious passion. I'd also much prefer to sit and read a book than get up and exercise, but I do try. Of course, I always feel better when I do. I don't deny myself anything, I just try to maintain a good balance between healthy food and drinks, and treats and desserts. It's important to remember that any step in the direction of a healthier lifestyle is a good step, and it always benefits you. That's one thing that is so exciting to me about health and nutrition, it directly benefits the doer, and it improves how you feel, look, and engage in life.

Living a healthy lifestyle isn't going to look the same for everyone. I enjoy yoga, whole grains, and dark chocolate, (okay, I'll be honest, any kind of chocolate is fine by me!). You might prefer basketball, protein bars, and fried eggs. Health, fitness, and feeling good doesn't look the same for everyone and it's not supposed to. God created us each unique, including our bodies and their needs.

Some of the things I like to do to maintain a healthy lifestyle are grabbing a bottle or tumbler of water every time I leave the house, buying fruit and vegetables every time I grocery shop, making a huge salad bowl and keeping it in the fridge for a quick lunch or dinner side, getting in a quick yoga session while my baby is asleep, and planning breakfast instead of defaulting to sugary cereal. Try different things and see what nutritious foods you personally enjoy, and what forms of activity you gravitate toward. A balanced diet, regular exercise, and adequate hydration and sleep, have a plethora of health benefits that will contribute to your most beautiful you. It's not about perfection. It's not about eating perfectly balanced meals 100% of the time, or obsessively working out 7 days a week. It's not about a diet, or being impossibly skinny, it's about a lifestyle of feeling good and being kind to yourself.

When I started taking better care of my body, I noticed a marked difference in my emotional state. I felt stronger, happier, and more confident. It may not seem like much, but the small, day to day decisions to care for yourself are empowering. They tell you that you are important. You are worth caring for. You're are valuable. And you are. God gave us these bodies to fulfill his purposes here on earth. Caring for them is not only a responsibility, it's gratitude in action. By caring for our bodies and being mindful that God's given them to us, as beautiful instruments of purpose, we are saying "Thank you, I appreciate this gift you've given me".

An area of health that isn't talked about as often as physical health is emotional health, but it's just as important as physical. Controlling our thoughts, or directing our thoughts, and caring for the wellbeing of our minds, is the groundwork for emotional health. Whatever you're entertaining in your brain is the directive for where your life will go. "Above all else, guard your heart, for everything you do flows from it" Proverbs 4 says. Whatever words are in your head are the ones that'll come out of your mouth. The attitudes you entertain are the ones you'll assume. The actions you consider are the ones you'll take. If you think negative thoughts, life will seem unfair and miserable. Only the things that are in your mind will manifest in your life. So . . . what are you thinking about?

I'm somewhat of a pessimist by nature. But I didn't actually realize that until I was a young adult. There was a period in my early twenties where I pretty much put myself into a semi-depression. I lived in a constant swirl of negative thoughts. I dwelt on the past, on decisions that I'd made and things I'd said, and beat myself up for my immaturity and lack of wisdom. I drove myself crazy with my helplessness and into dark moods with my negativity. I was very unhealthy emotionally.

By coming out of that self-inflicted depression, and other bouts of negativity, I've learned several things about emotional health and ways to maintain it. The first things I learned were - to accept my reality, and to put the past in the past. A wise friend, who has mentored me for years, would tell me "It is what it is." If something can't be changed, it can't be changed, and you'll drive yourself crazy trying to change it. The beginning of emotional health is accepting your reality, only then can you begin to deal with it. After that, let the past go. You can't change it now, it's over and done. Grieve over it, if you need to. Maybe you need to work through some things that still affect you. But, at some point, let the past go. Only by letting go of the past can you live in the present, and look to the future.

These next two go hand in hand, also. As I said before, I've been a pessimist for a long time. Someone once told me that if they pointed out a clump of flowers, I would reply that they were wilted. I am very prone to negativity, stress, worry, and tension. So, two of the major mental battles I've fought have been releasing negativity and choosing joy. Around the time I was slowly coming out of my semi-depressed period as a young adult, I made a decision. I'd been a negative, glass-half-empty person for over two decades, and I decided I didn't want to be her anymore. For the most part, (I definitely still have my depressed moments, okay, maybe days once in a while) I consciously let negativity go, and choose to be joyful. Now, that does not mean I am always happy. It does not mean I go around with a plastic smile, pretending things are okay when they're not. What it does mean is that I try to notice and appreciate the positive, like a vibrant sunset, my baby girls' laughter, a cup of coffee and some homemade muffins, a good book, a rainy day at home . . . I do things and take time for things that refresh my spirit. It takes some practice to get into the habit of looking for the positive, instead of dwelling on the negative, but it gets easier and more natural as you continue to do it.

Another way to choose joy is to practice gratitude. Some people do this by journaling, I do this, generally, by saying thank you. I pray and thank God for general things, like blessings and safety, and more specific things, like members of my family and the outcomes of specific situations. I also thank people, especially people who are close to and do a lot for me, like my husband. This practice is a powerful one because you cannot be negative and grateful at the same time. Try it, if you're being genuinely grateful, it's impossible to be negative.

In addition to looking for the positive and practicing gratitude, I monitor the internal dialogue. This has two parts: the constant internal discussion you have with yourself, and the imaginary conversations you have with other people. I don't know if everybody does this, but I would hazard a guess that many people do. Self-talk, specifically negative self-talk, is the silent conversation you're always having with yourself. You might look in the mirror while you put on your makeup and you tell yourself, for the thousandth time, how big your nose is. You may struggle to grasp a specific concept and then berate yourself for how stupid you are. You try to do a task as best you can, but when you make a mistake a little voice whispers "you'll never be good enough." Silence the voice! This is your battle to win. God said he's given us strength and peace and controlled minds.[1] We can do this! We are more than conquerors.[2] Create a habit of turning off the negative self-talk and replacing it with positive self-talk. What you replace it with, specifically, is up to you. Positive self-talk, affirmation, prayer, reciting scripture, redirecting to more neutral thoughts, reading, starting a conversation, finding things you're thankful for, are all ways to replace negative self-talk. I'm sure you can come up with plenty more. Find a replacement technique that works for you, or several if you want to, and replace the negative self-talk every time you catch yourself doing it. Don't let you be mean to yourself.

The other internal dialogue we must monitor is the imaginary conversations we have with other people that never actually happen. I catch myself doing this a lot. I may be stressed about something I need to tell someone, so I'll play out the scenario in my mind. Or, I might be upset with someone and have a silent argument with them in my head. I also have a tendency to read emotions into other people based on what I'm feeling. If, for example, I'm afraid someone won't like something I do, I instinctively start thinking and acting like they are mad at me. This is dangerous, too, because you can build up anger, resentment, or fear, against people for things they haven't said or done. That isn't fair to them, and can be hurtful to your relationships. If you constantly find yourself in hypothetical arguments with people, use your replacement techniques that we talked about earlier. Preparing for a conversation is great, but constantly fuming or getting emotionally charged over someone who hasn't done anything, isn't. Be sure, when you go into a conversation with someone, you start at ground zero, without bringing any imaginary emotions into the exchange.

Another way I find balance in my emotional life is to make time alone a priority. Our culture glorifies busyness. The internet and social media are constantly beckoning. Our lives are often filled to the brim with things to do. And if there's not much to do, we fill up the empty space with mind-numbing activities, like movies, TV, and Instagram. I get it, I love my Pinterest.

In our house we have "Quiet Time." Quiet Time originated from naptime. As my older daughter got to be around three years old, she didn't actually sleep during naptime every single day. So, we started calling it Quiet Time, letting her know that whether or not she actually went to sleep, this is a time to rest and be alone for a while. Some days Quiet Time doesn't happen, for various reasons, and I can definitely feel it when it doesn't. But I try to make it happen nearly every day. As a mom, I have come to depend on Quiet Time as an anchor of my sanity. With my personality, I need lots of time to reflect and be alone. Quiet Time is a place I can recenter myself, maybe get in some exercise, write, read, do a Bible study, a quick chore or two, or just sit still. That hour or two by myself is a breather that helps me do the rest of the day well.

I encourage you to find a few minutes each day to be alone. Even if it's just 15 or 20 minutes sitting outside, curled up in a chair, or out for a walk. Be alone with your thoughts, or use a creative outlet like writing or reading, or a physical one like exercise. You'll probably be surprised as you continue doing this, how much you look forward to it and how much refreshment it gives your spirit. Psalm 46 says, "Be still and know I am God". It's difficult to contemplate anything of meaning or importance if you're constantly rushing from one activity to the next. I think we all can benefit from more quiet time in our lives. Caring for one's mind is a very important part of wholeness and health. The Bible talks a lot about emotional health, we just don't think about it that way. In Proverbs 17:22 it reads, "A merry heart is a good medicine, but a broken spirit drieth the bones." In 1 Thessalonians 5:16 it says "Rejoice always." Also, Philippians 14:8 tells us that whatever is true, noble, right, pure, lovely, admirable, think about these things. I encourage you to care for your mind as well as you care for your body, because all of your life originates there.

Lastly, on the topic of health, is spiritual health. Spiritual health is the most important kind of health, because not only does it affect this life, it affects the next one.

A critical element in spiritual health is feeding your faith. Hebrews 11:6 says you cannot be pleasing to God without it. Of course, once you've been introduced to Christianity, the hearing of and reading the Bible is the next step to growing in faith. That's the best way to hear what God has to say to humans. Read and study it for yourself. It's great to get wisdom and perspective from older and more experienced Christians. But, at the end of the day, you've got to know what it says for yourself. No one else can do your studying or faith building for you.

There are many different ways to study the Bible. If you ask around or do a quick search on the internet, I'm sure you'll come up with a number of options to choose from. Studying is different from reading. When reading, we basically just pick up the facts of the text. Studying goes deeper and tries to unearth the meaning, context, application, definitions, and purpose of what's written. Studying is the search for the meaning behind the words, not just the words themselves. My favorite way to study is topical/inductive. I may have a word I want to understand better, or a broad topic, so I gather related scriptures, look at the Greek or Hebrew definitions of the words, maybe read different translations or commentaries about the topic, and make my observations. Beyond Bible reading and topical study, I like to study and read about extrabiblical evidence, anything from fossils pointing to a worldwide flood to secular historians giving supporting evidence of Christianity in Jesus' day. Some good resources that I've enjoyed are The Case for Christ, The Case for Faith, and The Case for a Creator by Lee Strobel, Mere Christianity by C. S. Lewis, and DVDs from Apologetics Press. There are many ways of studying the Bible, and some may appeal to you more than others. Here are a few methods to get you started:

SOAP Method

Scripture - Choose a verse or passage that you want to study

Observation - What jumped out at you? What do you want to study deeper? What is this passage saying? What did you learn?

Application - How can you apply this passage to your life right now?

Prayer - Pray for a good understanding of this scripture

Chapter Study

Choose a chapter of the Bible to study. Read it in its entirety. Scan the previous chapters for context. Go back and read the chapter slowly verse by verse. Try to find the main point(s) of the chapter, sections (if there are sections), who the speaker and audience are, time frame (when in history this is taking place), and how this chapter applies to you as a Christian today.

Word Study

Choose a word you'd like to study. Look at how many times this word is used in the Bible. Find the definition. Compare the verses in which this word is used. Is the word used literally or figuratively? How does this word translate in other Bible translations? Does this word apply directly to you?

I try to feed my faith both logically and emotionally, because as Christians, I think we need both. If we are totally and completely on logic's side in our Christianity, our hearts are cold and there is no relationship, only a transaction. "God, if you forgive my sins, I'll try not to do bad things." But if we are totally on emotion's side, we desire no reasoning or evidence, only warm, fuzzy feelings. "Oh, yesterday I just got this *feeling*, and knew it was from God, and then I got really warm and saw bright lights and heard lots of voices and I just know I'm saved from my sins!" We must base our faith on more than our feelings. Feelings are emotions and emotions are unstable and unreliable. They are no foundation for faith. We will give up on God as soon as our feelings leave us. "My dog just died and so there must not be a God, or He must not love me. If He did, He wouldn't have let this happen to me." Feelings can feel great, or they can feel terrible. But they won't stay the same, so we must have something steadier to rest our faith on.

There must be both logic and emotion. I rest my faith on the fact that there's both secular and Biblical evidence that a man called Jesus Christ lived and died by crucifixion, that His tomb was empty three days later, and that Christianity sprang from the Jewish religion. I rest my faith on the principle that Intelligent Design cannot come from anything but an Intelligent Designer. I rest my faith on the Bible being a self-supporting book, yet is still supported by history, science, and archaeology. I can't rest my faith on something that doesn't have logical evidence supporting it.

At the same time though, I mustn't be all about logic and forget that Christianity is about a relationship, the relationship between a powerful God and the people He made. When I am outside, and I revel in the beauty of a new day, the deep blue sky, pure sunlight filtering through the trees, and the wind caressing thousands of leaves, I am in awe of this Being that can create such beauty with finesse and precision, and my spirit worships Him. When I look at my daughters and see their miniature faces and iridescent blue eyes looking back at me, I am in wonder at a God that can craft such tiny beings with such absolute perfection, and my spirit worships Him. When I see the world's violence and hatred, and know that it is wrong, I marvel that the very fact that we know evil is evil is evidence of an absolute morality.

When I think about Jesus Christ being a historical fact, and doing unexplainable things like leaving an empty tomb and disciples willing to go to the death because they insist their leader is alive, and how those facts support the Biblical documents, when I consider the evidence and how well founded it is in historical accuracy, my logical side is overwhelmed and surrenders to the evidential weight of Christianity. And as I relent to the evidence again and again, I conclude that since this Christianity thing is real, then this God who hides himself to allow us free will, yet gives us plenty of evidence to compel us into making a decision, must be real and must love me and long that I respond to Him. Then I am humbled and my spirit worships Him.

Mark 12:30 says to love God with all your heart and all your mind as well as your all your soul and strength. Using only one of those won't work. God gave us reason, logic, emotion, intellect, passion, conscience, fervor, intuition, heart, and He expects us to use them all. He doesn't give us a gift and not want us to use it.

Christianity is not emotionless nor is it brainless. It is every single part of you in pursuit of truth.

Another element in spiritual health is perspective. Many people view being a Christian as something they do, not who they are. Church is somewhere they go, not the people they are a part of. God is a religion, not someone with whom to be in a relationship. Authenticity must be something that is important to us if we want to live genuine, healthy lives. If we aren't living authentically, then we are not being our true selves. We are not living, or are afraid to openly live, our beliefs.

To be authentic, our Christianity must be a very real part of who we are, not just something we do occasionally. I am not a Christian only on Sundays. I am not a Christian only when I do something good. I'm a Christian every day of the week because there is a God whose grace I need every day of the week. I'm a Christian every time I do something good, and every time I mess up, because Christianity is for broken, messed up people. I am a Christian at all times because that is a part of who I am, a broken, imperfect, perfectionistic, ambitious, striving, weird, beautiful mess that makes me, me. I am a Christian all the time, even in the messy moments, because God is God all the time.

Religion is just a word people made up to put God in a box, to get God out of things they didn't want Him in, like their lifestyle or politics. It's what people think and say and make up about what God wants, not necessarily what He actually has said He wants. God desires, not a religion, but a relationship with you. In Ephesians it says that God planned to adopt us before He even created the world, according to His pleasure and will. That means He wanted to! He was excited about it. Christianity is a constant relationship with somebody, not something we do on certain days or with certain people. I am in a relationship with my husband all of the time, not just when I'm spending time with him or when I'm with his family. Our Christianity must be real, it must be who we are, not just something we do or somewhere we go. It has to a part of us all the time. It's with you when you go to bed at night. It's with you on social media. It's present at your friend's house. It's with you on dates with your boyfriend. It's in your words when you talk to your family. Our faith must be real and present in our lives, or it isn't faith.

Something I strongly urge you to do, that has helped me hugely in my life, is find a mentor. Look for a woman you respect and trust, that is some years older than you, who is Godly and has lived life for long enough to offer you her wisdom and experience. I wish every young man and woman had a mentor. The woman I consider my mentor is such a wonderfully loving, Godly person. I knew her in high school, but grew close to her after I got married and started having kids. Our personalities are very similar, so we click well. She has taken me under her wing whenever I needed a listening ear or some wise advice. She has been there for me when I was confused, or angry, or crying on the phone. She would hear me out, whether it related to being a mom, a wife, or a Christian woman, and then offer me her advice, or sometimes, if I needed it, just a compassionate ear. We've had Bible studies together, talked scripture, moral issues, parenting techniques, hard decisions, ways to be a godly wife, and innumerable other topics. She has been such an irreplaceable friend to me. She has definitely lived out the Titus 2 scriptures that instruct the older women to teach the younger women. Find someone who will invest in you. The relationship between my mentor and I happened organically, but it doesn't have to. Asking a trusted, close, older woman in the church to mentor you in being a Godly young woman is an amazing thing. You could ask her out to lunch or to your house for a Bible study.

No matter what way you do it, please just do it! If not right now, at some point soon, find a mentor.

A last word on spiritual health, take some quiet time regularly to pour into your spirit and feed your faith. I call my ritual Coffee and Bible. I saw my mom do this all through my childhood. Every morning she'd drink a cup of coffee and read the Bible. I started doing it too, as a teenager, and then my siblings after me. For the most part, I've kept it up ever since. It seems to get the day started off right. If I don't take some time to reach out to and connect with God, or fill my spirit with His words, first thing in the morning, it feels like something is missing in my day. I'm usually more impatient and snappy at my children and frustrated with little inconveniences, because I haven't centered my mind on what really matters. I'm not at peace when I'm trying to control and micromanage every detail of the day and expecting everything to go my way. If I don't take a step back to look at the bigger picture, that I'm here on this earth to love God, love others, and love myself, then every little thing seems like such a big deal when it really isn't. Even just reading a short devotional and a few verses, not even thinking about the bigger picture, will bring your mind to higher things, and center your perspective. If I haven't taken time for God to pour into me and speak to my spirit through His Word, then I haven't given Him the chance to say to me -

Be still, just rest. I've left you my peace, don't worry. I've got this, it'll all work out for good. I've got enough strength and grace for you all day today. My mercies are brand new this morning. You can't imagine how big my love for you is or how far it goes. I'll be with you the whole day so don't sweat the small stuff, or the big stuff either. I'll take care of all of it, you just love me today, and give my love to others. Have a good day sweet girl. I love you.3

Now, if someone walked in while you were having breakfast and told you something like that, wouldn't you relax a little and feel like you could handle the day a bit better? That is what God says to us in the Bible, but we won't be able to hear it if we don't actually read it. He says those things and so much more, but we'll miss them if we aren't listening. Making a habit of Bible reading is a very valuable asset as a Christian. Do yourself a favor and start today!

Workbook

- Create a facial skincare routine (I like to cleanse, exfoliate, and moisturize)

- Find a kind of exercise you genuinely enjoy

- Make a list of new, healthy foods you want to try

- Do some self-massage (I massage my neck, traps, and shoulders by kneading, rubbing, pushing, and pinching the muscles with varying amounts pressure)

- Take a detox bath (I enjoy using sea salt, apple cider vinegar, and baking soda in warm water.) But don't do it too early in the day! It can leave you feeling weak and drained. Right before bed is ideal.

- Say affirmations to yourself

- Build a Quiet Time into your daily routine

- Start a gratefulness journal (Start by writing down three things you're thankful for from that day).

- Put an inspirational quote or Bible verse on your mirror

- Make your own version of Coffee and Bible

What They Said

A healthy outside starts from the inside.

- Robert Urich[4]

There's nothing interesting about looking perfect--you lose the point.

- Emma Watson[5]

A rose can never be a sunflower, and a sunflower can never be a rose. All flowers are beautiful in their own way, and that's like women too.

- Miranda Kerr[6]

Be careful how you are talking to yourself because you are listening.[7]

- Lisa M. Hayes

The real difficulty is to overcome how you think about yourself.

- Maya Angelou[8]

Nothing makes a woman more beautiful than the belief that she is beautiful.

- Sophia Loren[9]

Write It Down

1) What makes you feel beautiful?

2) What are some things you've been told about beauty?

3) Are those things true?

4) What are you doing right now to improve your physical health?

5) What is something you can do to feel good today?

6) What are you doing right now to improve your emotional health?

7) What is something you can incorporate into your life to improve your emotional health?

8) Is there something you need to let go of for your emotional health?

9) What are you doing right now for your spiritual health?

10) What element will you incorporate into your daily, weekly, or monthly faith building routine?

11) What resonated with you in this chapter?

12) Which Whole You tips are you going to do today?

Notes

My Go-To Recipes

<u>Breakfast</u>

-Oatmeal Applesauce Muffins

(Included with permission from the friend who kindly shared her recipe, with a little personalized tweaking from me.)

  1 cup quick oats

1 cup unsweetened applesauce

1/2 cup milk

  1 large egg

1 teaspoon vanilla

  4 Tablespoons melted butter or coconut oil

1/3 cup sugar or 1/4 cup honey

Stir together. Add:

3/4 cup whole wheat flour

  1/4 teaspoon salt

1 teaspoon baking powder

  1 teaspoon baking soda

Optional-

generous sprinkle of cinnamon, raisins, dried cranberries, or chocolate chips

Spray muffin pan or use paper baking cups before adding batter. Bake at 400 degrees until slightly browned on top. Makes 12 muffins.

-Overnight Oats

1/2 cup quick oats

1/2 cup milk (or enough to barely cover oats)

1/4 teaspoon vanilla

Sprinkle of cinnamon

Large dollop of honey or coconut sugar (adjust to your taste)

Optional-

banana, blueberries, strawberries, peanut butter, chocolate chips, yogurt, coconut, mango, (anything works here, follow your taste buds)

Mix together, top with desired additions, cover, and refrigerate overnight.

- Toast

Toast some whole grain bread. Top with choice of:

Peanut Butter and Sliced Banana

Hummus, Avocado, and Fried Egg

Hummus and Sliced Tomato, with salt

Mashed Avocado and salt

Nutella and Sliced Strawberries

(The possibilities are endless! Swap out the bread for whole grain bagels, English muffins, or waffles. Use lite cream cheese and jelly on a waffle. Make a sandwich with an English muffin, egg, cheese, and turkey bacon or sausage. Spread a bagel with cream cheese or Nutella and top with berries. Use your imagination and go crazy. Breakfast never has to be boring!)

Snacks

- Apple and Peanut Butter

- Refried beans and tortilla chips

- Mixed fruit

- Hummus and sliced veggies

- Vanilla Greek Yogurt (no sugar added) with fruit and wheat germ

Meals

- *Grilled Cheese with Hummus and Veggies*

Butter (or spread with coconut oil) two slices of whole grain bread on one side each. Spread inside with hummus. Layer with choice of cheese, sliced tomato, torn spinach, etc. Assemble and grill on a pan or griddle until cheese is melted.

- *Corn and Bean Salad*

Variety 1

Can (or previously frozen, cooked) corn

Can black beans

Tomato, diced

Avocado, diced

Cilantro, washed and torn off stems

Optional- pintos, black-eyed peas,

Olive oil

Apple Cider Vinegar

Salt

Mix together. Drizzle with olive oil, splash with apple cider vinegar, sprinkle with salt. Cover and refrigerate. Serve alone or with tortilla chips.

<u>Variety 2</u>

Can (or previously frozen, cooked) corn

Can black beans

Tomato, diced

1/2 cup diced strawberries

1/2 cup peeled and diced cucumber

Vinaigrette (or olive oil, apple cider vinegar, and salt)

Mix, cover, refrigerate. Serve as a side. (If you wanted to go slightly Greek you could always throw in some Feta cheese and scoop with pita chips!)

- *Burrito Bowls*

(Portion according to the size of your family, or the people you're serving.)

Hot, cooked brown rice

Choice of meat (shredded chicken, ground turkey, etc., or go vegetarian)

Choice of beans (black, pintos, refried)

2-4 veggie topping (cooked corn, diced tomato, sliced avocado, chopped mango, chopped lettuce, sliced peppers, whatever floats your boat)

Optional toppings: sour cream (I use plain Greek yogurt), shredded cheese, choice of salad dressing or sauce, tortilla chips, sprinkle of salt, salsa, guacamole, etc.

Serve in separate dishes and have everyone create their own, personalized dinner!

Chapter Five

Be Afraid and Do It Anyway
Facing Fear and Creating Confidence

I was trembling. I'd agreed to this, but I was trying not to be terrified. When I had accepted the request, I'd agreed with a smile, but my smile was gone now. People lined the gym, the bleachers full, and more people were standing up in the entryway. I took the mic when she offered it to me and tried to regulate my breathing. This is what I love to do. I do it all the time at home. So why did this terrify me and cause my body to convulse in shudders? I knew the song, and I knew I knew it. I'd done this before, shouldn't I be handling it better by now? Whether I should or not, my throat still decided to close up on me, and my breath control was shot. And you can't sing if you can't breathe. Why were a few pair of eyes so scary? No one was going to throw tomatoes or eggs at me. I wasn't going to die. So, why was I petrified? I took a breath and started to sing.

All of us are afraid of something. It may be mice, public speaking, getting abducted, or performing in front of an audience. We all have things we fear. For some, fear is stimulated by both internal things, as well as external. It seems like this kind of fear hits girls especially hard. We fear we are not good enough, we fear we're stupid or have no common sense. Sometimes people in our lives actually say these words to our faces, teachers, parents, coaches, peers, bosses, bullies, siblings, spouses. It could be anyone, under the guise of honesty or love, who cuts us down. They might think that they're just doing us a favor, giving us the "hard truth." Instead of building up and affirming another person, often a young and impressionable person, they will limit and discourage them, causing them to believe that in some way, they just don't measure up. That is so very wrong, because it's just not true. If we are the average human being, we have the intelligence and mental capacity to do nearly anything we decide to do (except things like fly or breathe under water, we don't have the capacity for those things, so please don't try). Sure, some jobs or activities or skills may be more or less suited to us, depending on our strengths, personality, and stuff like that. But that doesn't mean we cannot learn to do them, only that it may be more or less difficult for us. Most everyone has the capacity to learn practically anything they want. Yet, we struggle with this fear inside us called Doubt.

Doubt tells us we aren't good enough, that we'll never measure up. "Those people who told me that I'm stupid are right." "This person I love said I have no common sense, so I believe it." "My teacher told me I can't do it, so I guess I really can't." "He looked at me like I am completely dumb." "I'm never going to understand this."

Silence the voice. Doubt is a self-talk voice that talks really, really loud, screams even. He knows our weaknesses and our vulnerabilities. He targets just the right spots. He can make us believe whatever he wants if we let him. But he's a fraud and a lie. Doubt is a tool of Satan, and Satan is the Father of lies, according to John 8:44. Satan uses doubt, low self-esteem, lies, fear, whatever he can, to hold us back from reaching our potential and living a life of freedom and Godliness. But we don't have to let him. God says we are more than conquerors through him who loved us, we can do all things through his strength, we've been given spirits of love and power, controlled minds, and he's given us freedom.[1] Doubt is a form of bondage that we voluntarily live under. It keeps us trapped in a cage of fear. Hebrews 12:1 says to throw off every weight that ties us down and reach for the goal of Heaven. We cannot fully live in the freedom that grace gives us when we are crippled by paralyzing self-Doubt. Doubt leaves little room for hope or vision. Proverbs 29:18 says people perish without vision. When we live in a hopeless, negative state of mind we are living as someone already defeated. We've got to step outside this cage of Doubt and fear.

Perhaps we aren't totally trapped in a cage of fear, but we see ourselves in a doubtful light. I've heard people say "I'm not very smart" or "I'm only a housewife." Why do we say things like that? We've been given incredible brains and we have enormous potential, so why do we voluntarily throw our hands up and let Doubt win? You are not "only" anything. You are many things and you have the potential to be many more things. Don't side with Doubt and sell yourself short. Quit the negative self-talk, negative verbal talk, and the Doubt cheer leading parties.

You. Are. Amazing.

When I had my oldest daughter, I'd been the typical young woman who complained about how she looked and who called herself fat purely out of dislike for what she saw in the mirror. But, at that point, I decided I wasn't going to do that anymore. I didn't want to encourage and exemplify poor body image and low self-esteem to my innocent, impressionable baby girl. And to this day, I don't think she's once heard me call myself fat. I stopped that negative self-talk and pushed the doubtful light to the side. God is a powerful God and He can use you, don't let Doubt tell you that you are not good enough for Him. God's already taken care of that. When we down ourselves not only does it affect how we think and feel about us, it affects others, too. When you hear someone talking herself down, it makes you think less of that person.   It's difficult to respect or think highly of someone who consistently degrades herself. It makes you think less of yourself, too. You are, after all, a human being like them. If they're not "good enough," what would make you any different? The less we respect and value ourselves, the less respect and value others give us. Negativity breeds negativity and Doubt breeds Doubt.

Not only does devaluing ourselves affect others immediately around us, it can affect, or give a connotation to, entire groups of people. When a man says "I'm not very smart" that can cast a shadow on his entire family. Since children often repeat what they've heard, and retain imprints from childhood, the kids will grow up thinking they aren't very smart either. Consequently, they may never strive for excellence in life. Their father's voice of Doubt and negative self-talk has been handed down to his children, and they have been defeated before they ever knew they could win.

When a woman says "I'm only a housewife" she is not saying that she devotes her time and energies to the worthy calling of loving her man and training her children. She is saying "I'm not worth much in the world. I'm not valuable enough in these circumstances to be concerned with improving myself, my mind, or my education. Because I do menial tasks that is all I'm worth." No, No, and NO! You are valuable, and talented, and worthy, and intelligent. You are not given gifts and passions and dreams that God expects you to just ignore. Stop, I repeat, STOP tearing yourself down! What's more, when someone says something like that they demean an entire group of people. What we say affects us, what we say affects others, and what we say affects our children, or our future children. When you cut yourself down you degrade the person God made you to be. Don't do it.

Along a similar line of thought, sometimes other people throw a doubtful light on us, and we must realize that and reject it before it seeps into our hearts and becomes a self-destructive belief. I've heard men say, publicly, that women are subservient. That is not true. Women are not less than, less important, or less valuable than our male counterparts. Galatians 3:28 says that there is neither male nor female, for we are all one in Christ Jesus. While there are differences in our genders and our roles, there is no difference in our worth as human beings or as Christians. Genesis 1:27 reads "So God created mankind in his own image, in the image of God he created them; male and female he created them" (NIV). Right there, God tells us that both genders are created in His image. Both are valuable to Him. That does not mean that we are the same but that we are equal in God's sight.

Where some people get confused is the hierarchy that God has established in the home and the worship service. Colossians 3:18 says "Wives, submit yourselves to your husbands, as is fitting in the Lord" and 1 Corinthians 14:34 says "Women should remain silent in the churches." There has to be some kind of order or hierarchy for anything, be it a business, government, military, social group, worship service, or family, to run smoothly and function well. Have you ever been some place where everyone was trying to lead and the phrase "too many cooks in the kitchen" came to mind? Or how about when no one wants to be in charge and nothing whatsoever is getting done? For anything to function efficiently some kind of order must be established. That does not mean anyone in that order is worth less or is inferior to anyone else in that order. A boss is not worth more than an employee nor is an employee inferior to the boss, they simply have different roles.

I've also heard men talk about women's education or career, that it makes her think she has equal footing with or is superior to a man. Now, let's clarify here, women and men *are* equal, *neither* are superior to the other, they are simply different!

Let's also get clear about education. Education is not wrong. Education can be used to promote wrong ideas, or it can become an idol, but in and of itself, education is not wrong, but very needed and very useful. The places in the world where education is little or lacking is very evident. And when education is restricted or withheld, it's a form of control. Malala Yousafzai, in her book I Am Malala, talked about her stand against the Taliban's restrictions on girls' education in Pakistan. As part of their efforts of control, the Taliban promoted harsh restrictions on women and banned girls from going to school. This is what she said about women's freedom:

> I sat on the rocks and thought about the fact that across the water were lands where women were free. In Pakistan we had had a woman prime minister and in Islamabad I had met those impressive working women, yet the fact was that we were a country where almost all the women depend entirely on men. My headmistress Maryam was a strong educated woman, but in our society she could not live on her own and come to work. She had to be living with a husband, brother or parents.
>
> In Pakistan when women say they want independence, people think this means we don't want to obey our fathers, brothers or husbands. But it does not mean that. It means we want to make decisions for ourselves. We want to be free to go to school or to go to work.[2]

When a person's life is clouded by the darkness of ignorance, they cannot reach their God-given potential. Depriving a person of the right and the opportunity to learn is just wrong.

God does not give us brains and then expect us to forget we have them. How can we study, understand, and share the gospel effectively if we don't have the knowledge and skills that are necessary? In Acts 18, Priscilla and Aquilla heard Apollos preaching about Jesus and realized he didn't know the whole story. So, they took him aside and explained to him "the way of God" more accurately. In order for Priscilla to have done this with Aquilla, she had to have known her stuff. She had to have used critical thinking, had the wisdom, intellectual skill, and confidence to show him that he had a lot right, but that there was more.

In 2 Timothy 2 it says "Study to shew thyself approved unto God, a workman that needeth not to be ashamed, rightly dividing the word of truth" (KJV). In order to study we must know how to read, know how to study, and have the tools and critical thinking to do it. Education is necessary to knowing the Bible for yourself and accurately sharing it with others. It's also highly important in the world we are living in today. There are so many ideas and beliefs floating around out there, we must be able to decipher what is real and what is not, what is truth and what isn't, what is tradition and what is opinion, what is good for mankind and what is a bad idea. Education is needed and necessary. Given correctly, it's the difference between light and dark in a person's life.

When I say education, I mean all forms of education. In this day in age there are numerous ways to learn. There are online courses, self-directed studies, tutoring, community classes, trade school, college, mentoring and more. I'm a firm believer in an unending education and education being more than just school.

Also, it's important to realize that education is simply a tool. It is not inherently good or bad. It can be used promote great things or it can be used to manipulate people to evil things. We must decipher everything through the lens of truth.

Recognize Doubt for what it is, a mind trick of Satan's. It's a lie. We must learn to recognize the lies and discern the truth. In order to do that we have to take every thought captive, as it says in 2 Corinthians 10. So today, what lies are you believing? Are you believing the lie that you're not good enough? We talked about that in a previous chapter. God has given you, as a human being, innate value. As a kid of God, you have immeasurable worth because God died for you. You are insanely enough. Clear the lie and discern the truth. You *are* good enough, God has made sure of that.

Are you believing the lie that you're stupid? Have no common sense? That you'll never "get" something? That you "can't"? Are you reading what I'm writing to you right now? Then you're not dumb, or stupid, or lack common sense. Even if you couldn't read, if you have average intelligence, you could learn to read if someone taught you. If you can do that, then you have the mental capacity to problem solve, and problem solving equates to common sense. Don't believe a lie that insults your intelligence. What other lies are you believing? Recognize them and discern the truth.

Doubt is born of fear. We fear we won't measure up, so we doubt we will. We fear failure, so we don't even try. We fear embarrassment, so we hang back. We fear danger, so we play it safe. I know, I am a very fearful person. But do you know what I fear almost more than anything else? Regret. I am afraid that I will reach the end of my days and regret an unlived life. I am afraid of not trying to reach my dreams. I'm afraid of not doing my best to train my children. I'm afraid of not learning and growing and reaching my potential. I'm afraid of not seeking the truth and, so, believing a lie. I'm afraid of not loving my family. I'm afraid of not forgiving that person who hurt me. I'm afraid I won't make an impact in the world. I'm afraid my life will just be a blip in the ocean of humanity. I am afraid of failing to try. I am afraid of being too afraid.

Even in writing this book, Doubt has been yelling at me in the back of my brain. He's saying "Who are you to be writing a book? This book will never get out of your notebook or off of your computer. You struggle with or have failed at everything you're writing about. What if it's just not good enough? What if you just fail?"

I am afraid, in writing this book, but I'm afraid and I'm doing it anyway. My hope outweighs my fear. My hope that the things I have to say will help you or inspire you or encourage you, and the passion I have to make sure these words get to you, pushes me past my fear of failure. I believe in what I have to say, and I know that, if I don't say it, I'll live with regret. That's something I'm not willing to do, if I can possibly help it. I am afraid, but I'm doing it anyway. I hope you do, too.

I am afraid of many things: the dark, snakes, failure, public speaking, vulnerability, attack, abduction, my children hurt, I fear all that and more. But, more than all those things, I fear being too afraid, and missing out on the life I could live. Jesus said, in John 10, that he came so his people could have life, and have it to the full. We, as God's kids, are not called to an unlived life, but to a lived one, a full one.

So, this is my challenge to you, and to me - be afraid and do it anyway. That thing on your heart that you want to do, or think you ought to do, or that God is calling you to do, be afraid and just do it. If it's something you care about, something that's important to you, failure to try is still failure. What's the worst thing that could happen? Think about it. Does the worst thing that could happen outweigh the potential rewards of attempting it? Does the regret outweigh the risk? Only you can know. Weigh each side, consider it carefully. If it's not that important to you, the regret won't be much. If it is important enough to you, trying will mean more to you than just not failing.

Fear is an alert for danger. We fear snakes because we don't want to get bit. We fear bees and scorpions because we don't want to get stung. But, many times we are afraid of things that are not actually dangerous, they just don't feel very good. Often, though, we can learn from those things, and do better the next time.

It's not about not being afraid. I'm not sure that fear ever really goes away, it only lessens. So, it's not about eradicating fear, but overcoming it. That's called courage, or bravery, when you're afraid and you still forge ahead. It's courageous to stick your neck out and do something that people could judge you for. It's courageous to do the right thing when others aren't. It's courageous to stand up for someone else. It's courageous to stand up for yourself. It's courageous to forgive someone who isn't sorry. It's courageous to get hurt and still love people. It's courageous to live out your own beliefs. It's courageous to step out of other people's expectations of you. It's courageous to live free from Doubt and low self-esteem. It's courageous to be afraid and do it anyway. "Courage is not the absence of fear, but rather the assessment that something else is more important than fear." - Franklin D. Roosevelt

Be brave.

Be courageous.

Be afraid, and do it anyway.

Confidence means trusting in yourself or in something or someone else. So very many of us struggle with it. Confidence, or the lack there of, has plagued me for as long as I can remember. I believe many people struggle with confidence because of the lies of Doubt that Satan has put in our minds. When we doubt if we are good enough, how can we be confident that we are? The answer is, we can't. Until we discern the truth and deal with Doubt, we can't be very confident. But there is good news, and that is we *can* discern truth and deal with Doubt. We *can* uncover the lies and silence the voice. We *can* grow our confidence.

This one is hard for me to write about, because confidence is such a struggle for me. Although, I have definitely grown in this area. It's been a slow process, though, built bit by bit. Although I have a long way to go in my confidence journey, I want to share with you a few things I've learned so far. Hopefully they'll help you, too.

First, respect yourself. God put you on earth for a reason, don't apologize for it. Constantly apologizing for your opinion negates whatever you have to say. You have a voice. Use it. Constantly talking down to yourself only increases Doubt's volume. You are worthy. Don't try to diminish the value God has placed in you. You have a soul, a mind, an intellect, emotions, a mission, a voice. God gave them to you on purpose. Own them! Speak and think humble positivity toward yourself. If that's difficult, start by speaking scriptures over yourself. "His grace is sufficient for me, I am more than a conqueror, I am wonderfully made" etc. (For the complete verses see 2 Corinthians 12:9, Romans 8:37, and Psalm 139:14). Respect yourself. You are valuable.

Similarly, respect others, as they have value, also. Nothing shows the heart of a person more than the way they treat others. Truly, how a person treats someone else tells more about them than the other person. So, treat others well. I know we're all human, we're all selfish, sinful, and proud. We're not always going to treat others in a way that communicates to them that they are valuable and worthy. But we must try. Talk to people with courtesy, respect, and self-control. Respect is really just communicating to another person that you acknowledge their value, either as a human being, or as someone in their unique position. Respect doesn't mean kiss up, be a door mat, have no brain, give up all rights, or lose all your privileges. It's how you would treat a stranger. You'd say please and thank you, hold open the door, control your words and tone, be courteous. Often, we treat our own families worse than people we're never going to see again. It shouldn't be that way. Do you respect your parents? Do you use words and your tone in ways that tell them you are listening to what they have to say, whether or not you agree with them? Are you flippant and proud towards them, insinuating that you know better and couldn't care less what they think? Home and family is where you learn and lay the groundwork for all the relationships you'll ever have in life. Do you treat your siblings well? Or do you make them feel small, stupid, or unloved? How you talk to and treat others is a reflection of yourself. What are you reflecting?

On a similar note, don't allow people who love you and are close to you to disrespect you. If a family member or close friend talks to you in a downright rude, belligerent way, especially if it's a recurring pattern, it is not okay. Everyone has a bad day, everyone sticks their foot in their mouth once in a while, those things are dealt with and gotten through. But if someone who is close to you is a toxic person in your life, the issue needs to be dealt with. You can go to them in a humble spirit and have an honest conversation with them, explaining how their words and behavior hurt you and makes you feel. Perhaps they never knew or considered how your feelings are affected by their behavior.

And abuse is never okay. There are whole books on having healthy boundaries in relationships, so I won't go into it here. But if you're in a struggling relationship with issues like this, I strongly urge you to get a Christian book on healthy boundaries. Some common forms of abuse are: emotional/psychological abuse, which consists of someone purposefully hurting another person mentally through shaming, threatening, humiliating, yelling and other tactics; verbal abuse (a form of emotional or psychological abuse) happens when someone uses their words and body language to demean another person, including name-calling, put-downs, and unreasonable criticism; financial abuse is when someone restricts the use of money from someone else, including cutting off access to bank accounts, restricting access to financial information, and controlling where that person can work; sexual abuse includes anything from unwanted touching to forced intercourse or sexual contact with someone else; physical abuse is any physical harm or threat to another person physically including slapping, punching, kicking, and hair-pulling.[3]

Please don't allow yourself to be walked over. Stand up for yourself, in a safe environment, of course. You're a woman with worth and intellect and decision-making ability. A person who will not listen to humble honesty, who won't learn self-control from healthy boundaries, perhaps would benefit from having one less friend in life. And if you're in a dating relationship with someone who consistently disrespects you, despite what you tell them, please break it off. It's not worth it. Don't hope for the best. Don't wait for them to change. They've got the wrong mindset, and that will probably be difficult for them to change and impossible for you to. Save yourself some heartache and regret later on. Find someone who respects you.

Stand up for others. That takes bravery, and bravery invokes confidence. If you hear someone talking to someone else in an inappropriate, belligerent, or condescending way, say something or do something, in a way that is as safe as possible for you. If you see someone being bullied, do something about it. Be brave. Don't let a moment pass in which you'll regret standing by and not doing what your conscience is telling you to do. Use discretion here, though. Don't put yourself in the position to be someone's next victim. Sometimes, just being someone's friend is standing up for them. Other times, the situation may call for an authority figure to be notified to correct the situation.

On the flip side, don't be a bully yourself. In this digital age, bullying doesn't just occur on the playground or in the school bathroom. Cyber bullying is a real thing. It hurts just the same. The thing about cyber bullying is that it seems to be a sneakier, easier way to be cruel to others. It's easy to keep up a nice girl image and be a total jerk to someone online, all at the same time. On bullyingstatistics.org it says that "Over half of adolescents and teens have been bullied online, and about the same number have engaged in cyber bullying. More than 1 in 3 young people have experienced cyberthreats online. Over 25 percent of adolescents and teens have been bullied repeatedly through their cell phones or the Internet." If you have a need to tear others down to feel good about yourself, or to get satisfaction, you need to deal with your heart issues, because bullying is not the path to fulfillment. The same website states that cyber bullying takes many forms including:

- "Sending mean messages or threats to a person's email account or cell phone

- Spreading rumors online or through texts

- Posting hurtful or threatening messages on social networking sites or web pages.

- Stealing a person's account information to break into their account and send damaging messages.

- Pretending to be someone else online to hurt another person.

- Taking unflattering pictures of a person and spreading them through cell phones or the Internet

- Sexting, or circulating sexually suggestive pictures or messages about a person"

Growing up is hard enough without your peers telling you that "you're stupid, you're worthless, go kill yourself, you're so ugly, no one will ever love you, I hate you," If this is you, deal with your heart. Stop killing someone else's. Go to them and make it right. Bad girls don't win. Even if it looks like it in movies, bullies are always the losers. End of story.

Another way to grow your confidence is to live what you believe from your own study of the Bible, not others' beliefs or expectations. Growing up in a Christian home, it's easy to piggyback off the beliefs of your family and church culture. And, for a time, that's okay. But at some point, ownership must be taken for your own faith. This one is a bit frustrating for me, because I want to be on top of my game in everything, in every way, all the time. When it comes to faith, I want to be authentic, and have all my bases covered and all the topics studied and all the right theologies with everything down pat right now! While that is good and honorable, it takes time, study, and reflection to discern the truth and decide what beliefs you will personally own. So, give yourself grace, you don't have to have all the answers right now. But, while it is a process, I think it must be a continual one. Study for yourself, with other people, read other people's thoughts about a topic, and try to discern what is the truth, and what is tradition or opinion. While tradition feels safe and opinion is loud and easy to come by, neither will get you to Heaven, or bring you deeper in your relationship with God. Truth and obedience will.

Bravery also comes into play when owning your convictions. It takes bravery, and confidence, to question what you've been taught. It's a form of rebellion, but a right and natural, though perhaps painful, one. People don't like their beliefs, authority, or tradition questioned, but that is exactly what discernment is. It doesn't have to be, and shouldn't be, an ugly thing; but a mature, dignified ownership of your life and beliefs.

Just as it takes bravery and confidence to question others' beliefs and decide your own, it takes bravery and confidence to live those beliefs and reject their expectations of you. This is especially hard if you come from a background, or church culture, that has a tendency towards legalism, instead of living in the New Testament doctrines of grace, love, unity, and freedom. It will take confidence to decide what you believe, and bravery to live those beliefs. But authenticity is honesty, and we are called to speak the truth in love, as it says in Ephesians 4. How we live is a form of speaking, it communicates who we are and what we believe to everyone around us. So, live your beliefs, not others' expectations, and do it in grace for yourself while speaking the truth in love to others.

Another aid in confidence growth is to step outside the drama. There's always drama somewhere, in family, church, social media, or friendships. Usually it does nothing but cause hurt feelings, pride, talk, and strained relationships. Unless you're smack dab in the middle of it, get out. If you are in the middle of it, own your part, make amends, and try to make peace. You'll be more confident knowing that you yourself did the right thing and tried your best to resolve the situation. You can then be at peace with yourself. If you aren't in the middle of it, try not to get involved, unless absolutely necessary. Just stay away.

Sometimes, to stay out of the mess, you might need to create some space. Depending on the situation, this might mean avoiding, but of course being respectful to, certain family members, hanging out with different friends, getting off or limiting social media, or something along those lines. Remember, none of these things have to be forever, could be only for a little while. You'll be glad you saved yourself some headache and heartache in the meantime. Sometimes, the most loving thing you can do for others and yourself, is to love them from afar. The Apostle Paul said in 1 Corinthians 3 that divisions and quarrels mean we are worldly and acting like sinful people. Try to stay out of the drama. You will grow in confidence, knowing that you're taking control of your own direction in life, steering clear of some of its pitfalls.

Lastly, if you look good, you feel good. Now, this is not original with me. I'm not sure who first said it or where I first heard it. But it's true, and it's cool, because this will be different for everybody. I'll be honest, there are days when I don't get out of my pajamas. To be even more honest, I'm in my pajamas as I'm writing this, cup of coffee beside me, at three o'clock in the afternoon. Maybe I should be blushing, but I'm not. Sometimes comfort is the order of the day and that is A-Okay. But, when it's time to get things done, get out of the house, and go meet people, you'll be more confident knowing you are pleasing to the eye. Now, don't take me wrong here, I don't mean to say that you should dress to appeal to the lustful, wandering eye. There is a difference between dressing with taste and class, and dressing with seduction. What I am saying is to put up the PJs, put on some actual clothes, fix your hair, apply some make up, do whatever you do that makes you feel pretty, attractive, and ready to conquer the world, and then go out and do your thing (like, conquering the world!).

Probably most women wish for a wider, or nicer, selection in their closet when it comes to looking nice, but work with what you've got at the moment, you can probably change it up later. Some people might think that this doesn't, or shouldn't, have anything to do with confidence, that confidence should only come from the inside, from a beautiful heart, from being comfortable with who you are, from being true to yourself, yada, yada, yada, . . . Now, I don't necessarily disagree with those things, some of those things I do agree with. But I know that when I feel like I look presentable and pleasing to the eye, I'm better able to present myself to people. They don't say "dress to impress" for nothing. It gives me confidence to know that the message my appearance is sending to the world is one of respect and taste. To be honest again, I don't wear expensive or name brand stuff. I shop thrift stores and resale shops. But I do enjoy looking nice or put together when I go out. I've found that when I feel ready to meet the world, it's because I've prepared.

It seems like some religious people believe that the plainer (think shabbier!) a person looks, the holier or Godlier they are. Nothing is further from the truth! God is the one who created beauty and pleasure, and the eyes and senses to enjoy them with. Enjoying and appreciating those things isn't wrong.

Who gave us bright colors? God did. Who gave us the color red? God did. Who gave women lovely curves and luxurious hair? God did. Who gave us butterflies and rainbows and sunsets? God did. Who gave us nerve endings to feel the wind on our skin, or a hand holding our hand? God did. Who gave us taste buds to enjoy flavors like chocolate, avocados, and strawberries? God did. Who gave us dark eyes, light eyes, murky eyes, midnight eyes, sunset eyes, ocean eyes, caramel eyes, and eyes to see all the others eyes with? God did.

Beauty, and the love of beauty, is not bad. Dressing well, dressing up, looking nice, taking care of yourself, feeling beautiful and attractive, is *good*. It's not bad. What is bad is *only* caring about your appearance, to the detriment of everything else. What's also bad is beautifying yourself for the wrong reasons. Am I trying to make myself look beautiful (appreciating the femininity He gave me), or am I trying to snag a guy so I will feel like I'm worth something (relying on others for my self-worth)? Am I trying to make myself look beautiful, but at the same time being rude and ugly to everyone around me? Those are heart issues, not appearance issues.

In Psalm 45 it says "So shall the king greatly desire thy beauty". Reasons and attitudes can be wrong, extremity can be wrong, neglect of everything else can be wrong, looking beautiful is not. In Genesis 29 it reads ". . . Rachel had a lovely figure and was beautiful." In 1 Samuel 25 it says that Abigail was an intelligent and beautiful woman. Song of Solomon has numerous exclamations of "How beautiful you are, my darling! Oh, how beautiful!" Beauty is no sin. God gave it to us as a wonderful gift! Just remember that balance and attitude is key.

Workbook

- Do one thing you've been too afraid to do

- List some lies you've been believing and kill them by finding and writing the truth

- Dress up and make yourself look nice today

- Respect yourself - use your voice today and don't apologize for it

- Call out Doubt the next time he talks to you. Shut him down and replace his voice with an affirming truth.

- Choose a strategy (or several) to defeat negative self-talk

What They Said

There is nothing wrong with being afraid. It's not the absence of fear; it's overcoming it. Sometimes you've got to blast through and have faith.

- Emma Watson[4]

The most alluring thing a woman can have is confidence.

- Beyoncé[5]

The woman who does not require validation from anyone is the most feared individual on the planet.

- Mohadesa Najumi[6]

No one can make you feel inferior without your consent.

- Eleanor Roosevelt[7]

You gain strength, courage, and confidence by every experience in which you really stop to look fear in the face. You must do the thing which you think you cannot do.

- Eleanor Roosevelt[8]

Never bend your head. Always hold it high. Look the world straight in the face.

- Helen Keller[9]

If we all did the things we are capable of doing, we would literally astound ourselves.

- Thomas Alva Edison[10]

Every great dream begins with a dreamer. Always remember, you have within you the strength, the patience, and the passion to reach for the stars to change the world.

- Harriet Tubman[11]

Write It Down

1) What is something in your life you'll regret not doing?

2) Is there an area of drama in your life from which you need to distance yourself?

3) What is a lie that someone has told you that you believed?

4) What is the truth underneath this lie?

5) Is there a toxic person in your life?

Some books I recommend on healthy boundaries are-

Boundaries: When to Say Yes, How to Say No to Take control of Your Life by Dr. Henry Cloud and Dr. John Townsend

The Emotionally Destructive Marriage: How to Find Your Voice and Reclaim Your Hope by Leslie Vernick

6) What are some steps you can take to deal with this person?

7) What resonated with you in this chapter?

8) Which Whole You Tips are you going to do today?

Notes

Chapter Six

Potential not Perfection
Finding Mr. Right

Here's a news flash for you: there's no perfect guy (insert lightning bolt and dramatic music). If you think you've got one, hate to break it to you, you'll come to find out he's not. If you're looking for one, I'm sorry, you're not going to find him. If you've already figured this out, given up all hope, and crawled under a rock in mute despair of finding Mr. Right, there is hope. It's called potential.

Before we go on to discuss potential, I want to get something out of the way. And that is, that there is no Mr. Right. There is not a one, lone, single person on this planet who is perfectly crafted and tailored to fit you, your needs, and your desires, that God will bring from the ends of the earth right to you, because no one else is going to work since they aren't him. Mr. Right really isn't real. It's just a title we've coined to call the one we've already chosen, or the one we are going to choose.

We can choose to marry anyone. That means we can pick someone more suited to us or less suited to us, more Godly or less Godly, with more potential or less potential. If you're someone with a similar personality to mine, your head probably just exploded with screams of "Well, how do I know who to pick?! What if I make a mistake? What if I choose someone to marry and there's somebody better out there for me? If marriage is not a divine fate, and it's really my own choice, what if I do it all wrong?!"

First, chill. Second, if you're a faithful person committed to following God, He is at work in your life. Your marriage is a part of your life so He can work in that, too. He's God, He can do anything. Third, yes, if it's all your choice then it's all on you and that's scary. But it's also freeing. You're free to say yes or no. You're free to turn down that date. You're free to find someone with a more similar background to yours. You're free to find someone Godlier. You're free to make your own choice. That can be a scary thing, but it's a powerful and freeing one.

It's about potential, not perfection. How do you know who to pick? Well, you need to have an idea of who you want, instead of just drooling over every cute hunk that comes along. What are your nonnegotiables? What are the things that are most important to you in a man? As there is no such thing as perfection, you have to look for potential. (Yes, some guys have more than others!)

So, look for the potential in him that can grow into Godly, desirable attributes and character. How does he treat and talk about women? About his Mom? Does he study the Bible, or does he even read it? Does he have self-control and show you respect, or does he snap at, berate, and try to control you? Is he humble and easy to talk to, or does his ego get stuck in doorways? Can he see where he's wrong and say "I'm sorry"? Is he good with kids, or does he brush them off as annoyances? Does he respect your parents and appreciate your family? Is he relaxed and does he have good times with them? Does he use jokes and sarcasm to make you feel small, stupid, or ugly? Is he respectful to others, or is he a bully or have anger issues?

The habits, tendencies, and attributes you see in a person now, are probably what you'll see later. People change, but unless they have a radical experience or a major shift in their mindset, they change incrementally. What you see in him now is a very strong indicator of what you'll see later. So, what do you see? Use your head, not just your heart. Emotions are tricky things and they're never stable. You have to lead your heart, despite the cultural phenomenon of following your heart. See Proverbs 23:19 for more on that. Use your brain and discern the truth. Is he someone who'd be loyal to you and your kids? Does he work hard to make a living? What are his most important priorities in life? Do they line up with yours? Do you genuinely respect him as a person? Are you okay with the relationship dynamic? Does he treat you as an equal or as an inferior? Does he appreciate your opinions and value your input? Is he easy to get along with? Do you see your lives going in similar directions? Does he treat you well?

It's so easy to get caught up in the feelings of the moment. I remember. Emotions rush and surge, butterflies invade the place your stomach used to be, and you don't want to be anywhere else but with him, ever! You're having so much fun going on dates, texting or talking on the phone, and doing stuff together. You feel so important and seen and valuable. It doesn't feel like any of it will ever change.

But it will, because it always does. You'll either stay together and get married, or you'll break up and go your separate ways. Whatever you choose, it will be your choice. God can and will work in the lives of those who love him, according to Romans 8:28. But he isn't going to force you to do something you've chosen not to do, he's given you free will. Who you marry is up to you. Make a wise choice.

Desperate or Dignified

Let's talk about you now. What do you really want out of a relationship? Are you genuinely looking for a potential spouse? Or are you kind of bored, really wanting a recreational relationship? Are you seeking affirmation, value, and confidence, and you think a guy can give you those things? Do you think it's what you're "supposed" to do? You're 16, 18, 25, whatever age, and people are expecting you to have a boyfriend or get married soon. So, you just play along, even though you're not sure if it's what you actually want or are ready for? Do you not really know what else to do with your life, and you think that one option is as good as another . . .

In other words, are you desperate? I know the feeling of not being "enough" without a guy. I shared in the first chapter how I looked to my boyfriend and others for my self-worth. It didn't work for me and won't for you either. I will be transparent here, I didn't get into relationships for all the right reasons. I was looking for a spouse, yes, but I also "needed" someone for my self-worth and value. I thought that being Somebody's would make me a Somebody. I was not enough on my own. I was not a whole person. That's what I regret more than anything.

I've struggled with confidence, depression, and low self-esteem for almost as long as I can remember. Affirmation from others was my life source. Criticism and confrontation were very painful. Failure was like a death blow. So, I played it safe, tried to be likable, acted the good girl, attempted to be perfect. While that got me good grades, it didn't do very much for my self-esteem. Then my future husband came along . . .

My confidence and self-worth soared, and my depression drained away. I clung to him, because I thought he made me what I'd always wanted to be, "enough."

It's a dangerous place to be in, using other people as the source of your worth and value. Because, even if you feel like they give you what you need, it won't last, it can't. There is no way a person can make another person valuable. We can affirm each other, we can encourage each other, and we should! But placing your worth on another person's shoulders is an impossible load to bear. It isn't fair to them, and it won't help you in the long run. It makes you needy and clingy. You say and do desperate things to try to keep them. Because you're afraid to lose the source of your value. It's a very immature state to be in, especially in a romantic relationship.

It's taken me years, in slow, incremental steps, to mature and get out of this state of low self-esteem. It's taken me a long time to become a whole person. While I still crave affirmation, I don't need it as a life source anymore. It's very freeing, growing into a whole person. While I still don't manage confrontation well, and criticism is never comfortable, they aren't the end of the world. They are learning experiences and growth opportunities. It is so relaxing and exhilarating knowing that someone can dislike you, disagree with you, disown you even, and you're going to be okay, because your worth and confidence comes from God and yourself, and nobody else.

I don't share these things with you because I'm proud of them, but to give you the chance to learn from my mistakes. I don't want you to make the same mistakes I did, enter relationships for the wrong reasons, or struggle in those relationships because you aren't a whole person yet. I want you to be a whole, contributing force in your relationships, not the leech I once was. Don't do it backwards like me. Be Somebody before you're Somebody's.

Are you okay whether you're in a relationship or not? Do you "need" to be noticed by a guy to feel like you're acceptable? Are you a whole person by yourself? If you can honestly say you are a whole person, perhaps you are ready for a relationship if that's what you want. If you can't say that you are, please work on yourself first, before looking for a spouse, before dating. You'll be doing yourself amazing good, and him as well! There's nothing sexier than a happy, confident woman. As much as some of us struggle with choosing joy and being confident in ourselves, it's true. Remember, there's no rush. Marriage is forever, and that's a long time to live with regret. Be sure, when you are considering getting married, you're doing it for the right reasons, and marrying a man with the right kind of potential. Don't settle because you don't see anyone else on the horizon. Don't rush into regret.

The strengths and weaknesses you see in him now are very likely still going to be there after you're married. They'll be more exaggerated, though, because he won't be on his best behavior trying to woo you. Once you say I Do, he's caught you. If you don't like what you see now, get out of the relationship and move on. You can't change him. So many women have tried that, and it doesn't work. It's hard enough changing yourself, do you really think you can change somebody else? If you can't accept him as he is, move on. It's as simple as that.

Don't look the other way, either. Suppose you don't like something he does or a certain something about him, don't just hope it'll go away, and don't pray he'll get over it. Girl, I'm telling you, he is who he is and, at his core, he'll stay that way. Go into relationships with your eyes wide open, knowing what you see is what you get. Go into marriage with your eyes wide open, accepting him just as he is. Honestly, it isn't fair to go into marriage wishing he were different. Never stay in a dating relationship with someone who demeans you in any way. If they cannot see and respect your innate worth, and treat you like they do, they aren't marriage material, at least not at their present level of maturity. Marry someone you genuinely respect, someone you really do think highly of and admire. It would be very difficult to respect the position you put him in, if you can't respect the person he is. Also, is he easy to talk to? Marriage is a lot of give and take. It requires a lot of communication. Look for someone who is approachable, and easy to be around. A team can't work very well if it doesn't communicate.

So, don't look the other way. Your I Do is on you. Who you marry is your choice; a scary, powerful, freeing one, and it's totally yours. If you can't accept him and live with him as he is, move on.

It's your choice.

Make a good one.

Workbook

<u>Whole You Tips</u>

- What is nonnegotiable? What qualities are you looking for in a husband? Write them down.

- Think about who could mentor you in being a Godly woman. Ask her to lunch, to a Bible study, or give her a call.

- What do you see in your immediate future? Whether it's being single, dating, or married, write and describe how you can glorify God and bless others in your foreseeable future.

- If you're single, list what amazing things you plan to do with that freedom.

- If you're in a relationship, list the potential you see in him.

- Describe what it means to be a whole person.

- Look up the corresponding scriptures to these attributes.

<u>Potential to look for in a future husband</u>

Humble-James 4:10

Giving-Pro 11:25, Matt 23:11

Honoring/Respectful-1 Peter 3:7

Loving-1 Cor 13, 1 Peter 1:22

Mature-1 Cor 14:20, James 1:4

Easy to talk to/Approachable-James 3:17

Diligent/Hardworking-Eph 4:28, 2 Thess 3:10

Kind Eph-4:32

Hospitable-1 Peter 4:9, Rom 12:13

Fatherly-Eph 6:4, Duet 6:7

Spiritual-1Tim 4:15-16, 2 Peter 1:10

Faithful/Devoted to family-Eph 5:31, Rom 12:10

Patient-Eph 4:2

Forgiving-Eph 4:32

<u>What They Said</u>

Insanity: Doing the same thing over and over again and expecting different results.

- Albert Einstein[1]

I think when you are young, you are hoping that this person will be the right one, the one you are going to be in love with forever but sometimes you want that so much you create something that isn't really there.

- Johnny Depp[2]

None of us marry Perfection, we marry Potential.

- Robert D Hales[3]

<u>Write It Down</u>

1) Ask yourself "Am I desperate or am I dignified?" Write down your answer.

2) If you're in a relationship list your reasons for being in the relationship. Are they dignified reasons or desperate ones?

3) If you're looking for a relationship, do the same thing.

4) If you're dating, are you absolutely comfortable with the relationship dynamic?

5) Are you hoping your boyfriend will change? Are you looking the other way about anything?

6) Can you honestly say that you're a whole person, or on your journey to being a whole person?

7) What resonated with you in this chapter?

8) Which Whole You Tips are you going to do today?

Notes

Wrapping It Up

I wrote this book because these things have been on my heart for a long time. I have a heart for girls, and I know that there are girls like me who struggle with the same things I struggle with. I wanted to help them. I hope that the things I've said have encouraged or guided you in some way. I want to believe, with all my heart, that the struggles and dark periods of my life, the mistakes I've made, the hurtful things I've said, the growing pains and regrets I've had, are not for nothing, but are for me and for you to learn and grow from. I want to look back on my life and know that I gave what I had, I did what I could, I left it all on the field, and that I have no more regrets.

To you, my reader, thank you for reading this book. I hope it has helped you. To you, and every girl in the world, may we continue to become whole people, embracing our value and worth that comes from a crazy-loving God, and growing in confidence through accepting and loving ourselves. I applaud and champion you on your journey, as I travel mine, to be Your Whole You.

- Meagan Trayler

Let's Connect!

Hi! My name is Meagan Trayler. A little about me: I'm a Christian, wife, Mom, entrepreneur, author, music lover, nutrition enthusiast, chocoholic, singer, and visionary.
Your Whole You is my ministry to girls to inspire them to be whole, complete people in themselves, by knowing their God-given worth and embracing who they are, and developing a healthy self-esteem.

You can find me on:

Instagram

https://www.instagram.com/beyourwholeyou/

Twitter

https://twitter.com/meaganmonique93

Email

www.yourwholeyou@yahoo.com

Goodreads

https://www.goodreads.com/meagantrayler

Bibliography

Chapter 1

1 *Why thinking you're ugly is bad for you | Meahgan Ramsey.* TED Talks. *YouTube, Dove Self-Esteem Project*, October 7, 2014, Web.

2 Teen *Depression Statistics & Facts.* teenhelp.com. Web.

3 Preventing *Teen Suicide: Kids in Crisis.* Dr. James Dobson's family talk. Broadcast, Tim Clinton, Sep 7, 2017, App.

4 Genesis 1:26

5 Psalm 147:11

6 Yandoli, Kayla. *17 Empowering Emma Watson Quotes That Will Inspire You. BuzzFeed.com*, April 15, 2015, Web.

7 *YOU. thehillsarealiveblog.com.* Web.

Chapter 2

1 Lieberman-Wang, Lisa. *20 Inspiring Self-Esteem Quotes to remind You to Love Yourself AS IS. yourtango.com*, July 28, 2017, Web.

2 QUOTES. *goodenessgracious.com.* Web.

3 QUOTES. *goodenessgracious.com.* Web.

4 Nikolov, Cris. *20 Will Smith Quotes About Changing Your Life. motivationgrid.com*, September 20, 2013, Web.

5 Most *Famous Winston Churchill Quotes. therandomvibez.com.* May 16, 2017. Web.

Chapter 3

1 hsperson.com

2 5lovelanguages.com

3 Deuteronomy 4:24

4 Campbell, Julia Claire. *Why fit in? [PHOTO]*. *jcsocialmarketing.com*, February 11, 2012, Web.

5 *103 Inspirational Quotes That'll give You More of a Boost than Coffee*. *marieclaire.com*.

6 Carlson, Scott & Whitney. *SOCIAL MEDIA & THE FITNESS INDUSTRY*. *heandsheeatclean.com*, July 13, 2016, Web.

7 Igarashi, Hayley. *16 things Beautiful People Have to Say About the Unimportance of Beauty*. *zimbio.com*, May 20, 2014, Web.

Chapter 4

1 Philippians 4:7, 13, 2 Timothy 1:7

2 Romans 8:37

3 Psalm 46:10, Matthew 11:38, John 14:27, Matthew 6:25, Romans 8:28, Philippians 4:13, 2 Corinthians 12:9, Lamentations 3:23, Romans 8:39, Matthew 28:20, Mark 12:30-31

4 Shinners, Rebecca. *15 Quotes That Will Inspire You to Live a Healthy Lifestyle*. *womansday.com*, April 8, 2016, Web.

5 Scanga, Michelle. *The Most Relatable Fashion Advice From Kate Moss, Taylor Swift, & More*. *whowhatwear.com*, August 4, 2015, Web.

6 Jen. *LET'S TALK BODY IMAGE AND SELF LOVE*. *yourstrulyjen.com*, December 10, 2013, Web.

7 Montana *Daily Inspiration - January 6, 2017.* montana-speaker.com. Web.

8 Ahearn, Brianna. *35 GREAT INSPIRATIONAL QUOTES.* thefunnybeaver.com, Web.

9 *10 Famous Beauty Quotes That Are Inspirational.* hotbeautyhealth.com. November 19, 2009, Web.

Chapter 5

1 Romans 8:37, Philippians 4:13, 2 Timothy 1:7, Galatians 5:1

2 Yousafzai, M. and Lamb, C. *I Am Malala. Pages 158, 218-219,* New York, NY: Little, Brown and Company, 2013, Book.

3 Tracy, Natasha. *TYPES OF ABUSE: WHAT ARE THE DIFFERENT FORMS OF ABUSE? healthyplace.com,* reviewed by harry Croft, MD, Updated: November 14, 2016, Web.

4 Kliest, Nicole. *12 Emma Watson Quotes That Every Woman Should Read. whowhatwear.com,* February 26, 2016, Web.

5 Walter, Liza. *12 Quotes From Inspiring Women In Honor Of International Women's Day. yourtango.com,* March 8, 2017, Web.

6 H., Felix. *100 Inspirational Quotes Every Woman Should Read. lifehack.org,* Web.

7 Mac. *Interesting and beautiful quotes (32 photos). thechive.com,* July, 2, 2014, Web.

8 Schroeder, Manda. *ROUGH, TOUGH. I'LL SUCK IT UP. weandserendipity.com,* March 13, 2013, Web.

9 Luc, Helen. *25 ways To Convince Yourself That You've GOT This. yourtango.com,* December 9, 2016, Web.

10 Olive. *Presents for You:* Brush *Lettered Edison Quote.* *randomolive.com,* November 21, 2014, Web.

11 Chavez, Rocio. *Let Go, Dream Bigger.* *yoursassyself.com,* August 9, 2017, Web.

Chapter 6

1 *Albert Einstein Quotes. parentpalace.com,* September 2, 2012, Web.

2 *When you are young, you are hoping that this person will be the right one, the one you are going to be in love with forever but ... heartfeltquotes.blogspot.com*

3 dailyensign. *None of us marry Perfection, we marry Potential - Robert D Hales. instagram.com*

Made in the USA
Lexington, KY
12 June 2019